Glorious End Times
for Christians

Steve Gravett

O&U
Onwards & Upwards

Onwards and Upwards Publishers

4 The Old Smithy, London Road, Rockbeare,
EX5 2EA, United Kingdom.
www.onwardsandupwards.org

First edition, published in the United Kingdom by Onwards and Upwards Publishers (2021).

ISBN: 978-1-78815-593-9
Typeface: Sabon LT

The views and opinions expressed in this book are the author's own, and do not necessarily represent the views and opinions of Onwards and Upwards Publishers or its staff.

Endorsements

Steve has done it again! He has set his proven and forthright authorship skills to the subject of eschatology; bringing clarity, profound understanding and depth to the subject of biblical prophecy.

The timing of this book is impeccable. The present global calamities of pandemics, financial market, arms races, political, racial and national tensions bring into sharp focus the context and content of this book. The book is a straightforward 'no nonsense' guide to the end times. It is a must-have resource for all Christians seeking to navigate the uncertainties of the present and embrace God's promises for the future. But, you don't so much read this book as you enter into a commitment with it. This is one of those rare gems that grows even more precious as the reader takes time to let all that is written sink in.

More importantly, Steve offers the Truth in a simple, unassuming way. There is no agenda, and hardly any 'eschatological' jargon.

The content of this book tackles subjects that are both fascinating and frightening for any reader. They point to key questions people have wrestled with for centuries, including:

- What does the Bible tell us about the future?
- How much can we understand about biblical prophecy and its application in our lives?
- What signs and signals will precede the end of everything as we know it?
- Which of those signs and signals have already come to pass? Which are we experiencing now? Which are still to come?

In *Glorious End Times for Christians,* Steve unveils answers to these questions and much more. Enjoy!

Ian Winter
Senior Manager for BAE Systems KSA;
Senior Pastor for a network of underground churches
in the Middle East

Steve has a gift for taking an important but complicated topic and helping the reader navigate through its different twists and turns to come to a better understanding. He achieves this by thorough research and clear thinking without over-simplification.

I warmly recommend this book to you.

Rev. Jonathan Snell
Retired Assemblies of God Minister
Sandown, Isle of Wight

Ever since the foundations of the early church, there has been great interest in the interpretation of the imagery and accounts found in the last book of the New Testament, the Revelation of John. As Christians, we are intrigued and fascinated with stories of the end times.

Further, with the recent worldwide catastrophes of disease, flood, earthquake and fire there has never been a time when there has been such detailed interest in the return of Christ and its realities for the Church.

As such, Steve Gravett's straightforward attempt to point us in the right direction through his book, *Glorious End Times for Christians,* is a welcome addition to the lexicon and a timely reminder for us all to be looking upwards.

The treatment of the messages to the churches remains particularly apposite and each chapter concludes with a number of thought-provoking questions.

Although a consensus of opinion about the details of such topics might arguably prove elusive, Steve's passion and insight help inform a balanced opinion on the principles of eschatological verification, including the parousia and its foreshadowings. There will be something here of value for bible scholars and lay people alike.

Dr Trevor Lee
Strategist and Educator
St Albans, Herts.

Along with Steve's other two Christian books, I find *Glorious End Times for Christians* incredibly informative and helpful. It is good for me, a non-academic, to have guidance on what the Scripture says rather than man's interpretation of it.

It gives a real enthusiasm and urgency in telling people that Christ has died, He has risen and He is coming again soon.

Les Tidball
Former British Director of Romanian Missionary Society

About the Author

 Steve Gravett was brought up by Christian parents; he accepted Jesus Christ as his personal saviour at the age of six and has been a committed practising Christian ever since. Steve has been involved in church ministry in a variety of leadership roles with children, young people and adults. He has also been a member of the Full Gospel Businessmen UK and Ireland, in the local Isle of Wight branch, and is a member of Go International (formerly the Gideons). He actively supports the Society of the Protection of Unborn Children, Open Doors and Release International.

Steve is a professionally qualified social worker (CQSW) and Manager (DMA) and joined Her Majesty's Prison Service where he worked as a Prison Governor for twenty-six years, throughout the UK. Over a period of four years he wrote a regular column for *Community Care* and has published five professional books. Since retiring and moving to the Isle of Wight in 2018, Steve has published three Christian books.

To contact the author, please visit his website:
www.steveauthor.co.uk

or Facebook page:
www.facebook.com/steve.author.73

or send an email to:
stevegravett2@gmail.com

More information about the author can also
be found on the book's web page:
www.onwardsandupwards.org/glorious-end-times-for-christians

Acknowledgements

I am grateful and appreciative of all the encouragement and assistance I have received from many Christian friends, who have offered advice, guidance and suggestions for improving the manuscript, for which I am very grateful. Special thanks to the Rev. Colin Le Noury, General Director, Prophetic Witness Movement International for kindly agreeing to write the Foreword.

I would like to thank the following people who have given me permission to use certain works:

- My niece Gillian Rickards for permission to use her poem *In Troubled Times;*
- My brother-in-law Alec Prowse (in his 95th year) for permission to use his poem *Rapture;*
- The Full Gospel Businessmen UK and Ireland for permission to use *Postscript;*

and also:

- My son Jonathan Gravett for designing and maintaining the website: *www.steveauthor.co.uk*

To Beryl, my lovely, exceptional and loyal
wife, with whom I celebrated fifty years of
marriage in 2020,

our three inspiring children,
Jonathan, Joy and Faye,

Simon, our much-loved son-in-law,

and our wonderful grandchildren, Zachary,
Ava, Laylee, Kai, Harry and Poppy.

Contents

"All scripture is inspired by God and is useful for teaching, for reproof, for correction, and for training in righteousness."

2 Timothy 3:16 (NRSV)

"I believe the Bible to be the inspired, the only infallible, authoritative Word of God."

Steve Gravett

Preface

Dear Reader,

The book of Revelation is one of the most exciting and absorbing books in the Bible. It contains the unveiling of the truth about end time events which is the "the word of God and the testimony of Jesus Christ" (Rev.1:2).

This prophecy contains the most horrific and frightening events in the history of the world that are coming soon for those who have rejected the Lord Jesus Christ. The prophet Joel warned, "Let all who live in the land tremble, for the day of the LORD is coming." (Jl.2:1)

It also unveils the most glorious and incredibly exciting future that is waiting for 'born again' Christians. This prophecy was given to inform us of future events and not to satisfy our curiosity; rather, to motivate us to take the Great Commission more seriously as time is running out. "He which testifieth to these things saith, Surely I come quickly." (Rev.22:20, KJV)

Unlike the New Testament Gospels and epistles, which are inspired by the Holy Spirit, this book is a direct communication and an eye-witness account of what the Lord Jesus Christ revealed to the apostle John. It contains the last words of Jesus Christ to encourage, reassure and inform 'born again' believers of God's future judgement. Someone's parting words, particularly if you do not expect to see them again in your lifetime, are often memorable because the speaker is sharing something that is personal to you. When those words come directly from Jesus Christ it would be foolish not to attach great significance to what he says.

Satan does not want believers to read the book of Revelation because it makes clear he will be defeated and ignominiously "thrown into the lake of burning sulfur" (Rev.20:10).

Given this unveiling provides an unique insight into the future, it is surprising that so many churches avoid this teaching that sets out the sequence of future events clearly. Its contents and imagery have generated considerable debate amongst students of eschatology, but it should not cause confusion, as it acts as the final chapter or executive summary to the other sixty-five books.

Prayerful study will reveal the truth contained within this prophecy. It should be borne in mind, Jesus told John not to write down certain things he witnessed, for reasons we are not told.

The book of Revelation is not an easy book to understand if you read it in isolation, as it presents a challenge to the reader much like a jigsaw puzzle; the pieces do not always fit together neatly, but as you persevere, you begin to see the full picture.

Many scholars try to interpret the book of Revelation but this can lead to serious error and misunderstanding. In this book I attempt to explain the meaning of this wonderful prophecy in simple terms without introducing my own ideas and theories. The late Dr David Cooper (1886-1965) provides this 'golden rule of interpretation' for understanding the many signs and symbols in the book of Revelation:

> *When the plain sense of scripture makes common sense, seek no other sense; therefore, take every word at its primary, ordinary, usual, literal meaning unless the facts of the immediate text, studied in the light of related passages and axiomatic and fundamental truths, clearly indicate otherwise.*
>
> Dr David L. Cooper
> *The World's Greatest Library Graphically Illustrated (1942)*

My own approach is to prayerfully read the Bible and "take to heart what is written in it, because the time is near" (Rev.1:3).

The book of Revelation was written for ordinary, uneducated people to understand. Whilst some symbolism is used (which I explain as we go along) this approach has led me to conclude that the sequence of future events set out in Chapter 1 is rational and scripturally accurate.

The contents of my book are self-explanatory, other than to mention that the letters to the seven churches have been placed at the end of the book next to the Postscript. This provides simple guidance for anyone challenged by this prophecy to become a Christian. It contains a prayer for those who admit they are sinners and are seeking forgiveness, and believe Jesus has paid the price for their sin. When you repent and make Jesus Christ the Lord of your life, you receive the gift of eternal life and the assurance your sins are forgiven.

God bless you.

Steve Gravett

Foreword by Rev. Colin Le Noury

The Book of Revelation is a fascinating book which gives us a clear window on Bible prophecy and end time events. This new work by Steve Gravett opens that window widely.

The author has done well in his interpretation and exposition of the glorious truths contained in this important Biblical book. He has not shunned from commenting on some of the very difficult passages which are sometimes controversial and other times hard to understand. His use of historical facts and of scientific data adds a great deal of credibility to our understanding of the prophecies, and illustrates his exposition admirably.

The book is written from a premillennial and pre-tribulational perspective which makes it very desirable at a time when works of alternate interpretation abound. Another strong feature of the work is the author's use of Old Testament prophecies which are shown to tie in with the prophecies of Revelation. This surely helps to underpin the veracity of these prophecies, often disputed by liberal theology.

The structure of the book is quite unique in that I haven't read an exposition of Revelation presented in this way before. As a Futurist, the author well understands the chronology of the Book of Revelation but he bypasses it somewhat, starting with the Rapture, which doesn't actually occur until Revelation chapter 4, and proceeds with his exposition from there. Having completed his exposition he then flashes back to the opening three chapters of Revelation. This is cleverly done so that the challenges to the seven churches (and to the reader) come after the foundational truths have been well laid.

The Book of Revelation itself promises a blessing to all who read and understand it. In this work, Steve Gravett enables us all to be partakers of that blessing. I hope it will be widely read and that the challenges to both believer and unbeliever are heeded.

Rev. Colin Le Noury
General Director
Prophetic Witness Movement International

Key to Translations

AMP	Amplified Bible
KJV	King James Version
NIV	New International Version
NLT	New Living Translation
NRSV	New Revised Standard Version

CHAPTER ONE

The Premillennial Rapture is Coming Soon

Introduction

Many people like to consult their horoscopes or an almanac to find out what the future has in store for them. They consider this to be harmless fun, but the Bible instructs us:

"Do not practice divination or seek omens."

Leviticus 19:26

However, if you really want to know what the future holds, then studying the Bible will enable you to discern the truth about the future. This book contains what God, the Creator of the universe, has already decided is our future and provides reassurance in a troubled world that God is in complete control of world events.

No scholars pretend unravelling God's plans for the human race in the book of Revelation is easy to understand, which may be why many churches and believers avoid this book altogether. Some theologians mistakenly believe these last prophetic words of Jesus in the book of Revelation are figurative and not to be taken literally, but this revelation of future events should be examined carefully as it contains serious warnings. It is inevitable this prophecy contains some symbolism because it is a huge challenge to describe events that will occur two thousand years in the future. How would you describe nuclear weapons, television broadcasts, or technological innovations like the computer or mobile phone? Consider the difficulty of describing modern air travel – a mysterious metal tube that carries hundreds of people safely through the air at great speed!

Many of the prophecies made about Jesus Christ, the coming Messiah, made centuries before he was born, contain some imagery. The language used was specific, intended to be taken literally and described future events with complete accuracy.

7

For to us a child is born,
to us a son is given,
and the government will be on his shoulders.
And he will be called
Wonderful Counsellor, Mighty God,
Everlasting Father, Prince of Peace.
Of the greatness of his government and peace
there will be no end.
He will reign on David's throne
and over his kingdom,
establishing and upholding it
with justice and righteousness
from that time on and forever.

Isaiah 9:6-7

Israel is Restored

The prophet Isaiah prophesied 2,700 years ago that Israel would be restored to their own land.

From 587 BC to the formation of the present day State of Israel in 1948 – that's 2535 years in all – the Jews were not in control of their nation or national sovereignty.

Phil Davies[1]

Yet in a single day on 14 May 1948 the state of Israel was reborn, which fulfilled the prophecy down to the last detail.

"Who has ever heard of such things?
Who has ever seen things like this?
Can a country be born in a day
or a nation be brought forth in a moment?"

Isaiah 66:8

Most people who are not Christians have no knowledge of a coming event called the Rapture which is when Jesus Christ promised to return to take believers into heaven.

Two thousand years ago Jesus Christ told his disciples he would return to earth and he identified seven signs that must be fulfilled before

---

[1] *The Miracle That Is Israel*

the Rapture takes place. There are no further signs to be fulfilled before the Rapture. The Greek verb *harpagisometha* means 'we shall be caught up' and the Greek word *harpazo* means 'to snatch away' or 'seize' from earth into the air.

Jesus Christ reveals to us in astonishing detail that sometime soon, when we least expect it, "the day of the Lord will come like a thief in the night" (1 Thess.5:2). He will return to earth as promised in the scriptures, then all those who are "born again" (Jn 3:3) – that is, those believers who have confessed they are sinners, have been forgiven and have accepted Jesus Christ as their personal saviour – will be raptured and will meet the Lord in the air (see 1 Thess.4:17).

End Times Signs

Each of the synoptic Gospels describes the signs that must take place before the return of Jesus Christ. In Matthew 24:6-8, Mark 13:5-8 and Luke 21:9-11, Jesus explained to his disciples at the Mount of Olives discourse these end times signs.

> *"But about that day or hour no one knows, not even the angels in heaven, nor the Son, but only the Father."*
>
> *Matthew 24:36*

These are the seven signs Jesus said must take place before his return:

- false messiahs;

> *"Watch out that no one deceives you. For many will come in my name, claiming 'I am the Messiah,' and will deceive many."*
>
> *Matthew 24:4-5*

- wars and rumours of wars;

> *"You will hear of wars and rumors of wars, but see to it that you are not alarmed. Such things must happen, but the end is still to come."*
>
> *Matthew 24:6*

- great earthquakes, famines and pestilences;

"There will be great earthquakes, famines and pestilences in various places, and fearful events and great signs from heaven."

Luke 21:11

- universal persecution;

"Then you will be handed over to be persecuted and put to death."

Matthew 24:9

- anti-Semitism;

"You will be hated by all nations because of me."

Matthew 24:9b

- worldwide evangelism;

"And this gospel of the kingdom will be preached in the whole world as a testimony to all nations, and then the end will come."

Matthew 24:14

- false prophets will deceive believers.

"At that time if anyone says to you, 'Look, here is the Messiah!' or, 'There he is!' do not believe it. For false messiahs and false prophets will appear and perform great signs and wonders to deceive, if possible, even the elect. See, I have told you ahead of time."

Matthew 24:23-25

Jesus warns believers concerning all these signs:

"These are the beginning of the birth pains."

Mark 13:8

Until Jesus Christ returns, the apostle Paul warns believers to be prepared as the wickedness and ungodliness of mankind will increase in the days prior to the return of Jesus Christ.

"But mark this: There will be terrible times in the last days. People will be lovers of themselves, lovers of money, boastful, proud, abusive, disobedient to their parents, ungrateful, unholy, without love, unforgiving, slanderous, without self-

control, brutal, not lovers of the good, treacherous, rash,
conceited, lovers of pleasure rather than lovers of God –
having a form of godliness but denying its power. Have
nothing to do with such people."

2 Timothy 3:1-5

The Coming Rapture

Before his ascension to heaven Jesus assured his disciples he would be making preparations for them in heaven.

> *"My Father's house has many rooms; if that were not so,*
> *would I have told you that I am going there to prepare a place*
> *for you? And if I go and prepare a place for you, I will come*
> *back and take you to be with me that you also may be where*
> *I am."*

John 14:2-3

THE PROMISES

Jesus Christ promised to return for all believers who have been "born again" (Jn.3:3) and have received his free gift of salvation. They are those who have confessed they are sinners, who believe Jesus is the Son of God who died on the cross to pay the price for their sins and have asked for and received His forgiveness. Everyone who has received Jesus Christ as their personal saviour has the assurance of eternal life and can look forward with confidence to the day Jesus Christ returns to rapture the church and believers.

> *Christ was sacrificed once to take away the sins of many; and*
> *he will appear a second time, not to bear sin, but to bring*
> *salvation to those who are waiting for him.*

Hebrews 9:28

The eternal future of those who have been born again is secure; they will spend it in heaven with him. "Now we are children of God" (1.Jn.3:2) we have been adopted into God's family.

> *Now if we are children, then we are heirs – heirs of God and*
> *co-heirs with Christ, if indeed we share in his sufferings in*
> *order that we may also share in his glory.*

Romans 8:17

But our citizenship is in heaven. And we eagerly await the Savior from there, the Lord Jesus Christ, who by the power that enables him to bring everything under his control, will transform our lowly bodies so that they will be like his glorious body.

Philippians 3:20-21

No Wrath for Believers

All Christians are promised they will not experience the wrath of God and they should not be afraid of "the face of him who sits on the throne and from the wrath of the Lamb" (Rev.6:16).

The judgement of Jesus Christ is reserved for those who remain unbelievers as the apostle John makes clear.

"Whoever believes in the Son has eternal life, but whoever rejects the Son will not see life, for God's wrath remains on them."

John 3:36

Jesus Christ has promised believers they will not go through the time of Great Tribulation[2] as he is going to rescue believers from that terrible time of suffering and distress when God unleashes his wrath on this sinful world.

They tell how you turned to God from idols to serve the living and true God, and to wait for his Son from heaven, whom he raised from the dead – Jesus, who rescues us from the coming wrath.

1 Thessalonians 1:9-10

For God did not appoint us to suffer wrath but to receive salvation through our Lord Jesus Christ. He died for us so that, whether we are awake or asleep, we may live together with him.

1 Thessalonians 5:9-10

---

[2] See p.22

The Rapture of Believers

The Rapture of the Church should not be confused with the Second Coming of Jesus Christ, which is an entirely separate event. The signs Jesus Christ warned his disciples about concern the end times and relate to his Second Coming. The Rapture of what Jeff Kinley describes as "the authentic followers of Jesus Christ"[3], when believers meet the Lord in the clouds, occurs at least seven years earlier. It takes place before the Second Coming of Jesus Christ and is an event that is imminent, meaning there are no prophecies left to be fulfilled. This explains why believers must be prepared for the Rapture to take place at any time without warning. There is absolutely no reason why Jesus Christ cannot return anytime when we least expect it!

The apostle Paul sets out the sequence of events that will occur at the Rapture of the Church. First of all, those believers who have died will be raised from the dead. Then believers alive at the time of the Rapture will be caught up to meet the Lord in the "clouds" and taken to be with Him in heaven for eternity.

> According to the Lord's word, we tell you that we who are still alive, who are left until the coming of the Lord, will certainly not precede those who have fallen asleep. For the Lord himself will come down from heaven, with a loud command, with the voice of the archangel and with the trumpet call of God, and the dead in Christ will rise first. After that, we who are still alive and are left will be caught up together with them in the clouds to meet the Lord in the air. And so we will be with the Lord forever.
>
> *1 Thessalonians 4:15-17*

When the Rapture occurs, we will all be changed from our earthly, perishable bodies, which have been contaminated by sin and have deteriorated due to the ageing process or disease, into our perfect, immortal bodies.

> Listen, I tell you a mystery: We will not all sleep, but we will all be changed – in a flash, in the twinkling of an eye, at the last trumpet. For the trumpet will sound, the dead will be raised imperishable, and we will be changed. For the

---

[3] Jeff Kinley; *As it Was in the Days of Noah*; p.74

*perishable must clothe itself with the imperishable, and the
mortal with immortality.*

1 Corinthians 15:51-53

When Jesus Christ returns to rapture the church, this transformation
will take place.

*But we know that when Christ appears, we shall be like him,
for we shall see him as he is.*

1 John 3:2

THE RAPTURE OF CHILDREN UNDER GRACE

The Rapture will come as an enormous shock to those left behind,
particularly to unbelievers whose children have not reached the age of
responsibility and accountability, as they will disappear too. Although
the Bible does not specifically elaborate on the position regarding
innocent children at the Rapture, Jesus was forthright in his condemnation of anyone who led precious children astray concerning
spiritual matters. He considered this to be such a heinous crime, it would
be preferable for anyone leading a child astray to pay for this crime by
being thrown into the sea with a heavy weight attached, so they would
be certain to die from drowning.

*"Things that cause people to stumble are bound to come, but
woe to anyone through whom they come. It would be better
for them to be thrown into the sea with a millstone tied around
their neck than to cause one of these little ones to stumble."*

Luke 17:1-2

It is apparent that Jesus regards children as very special to him. When
some parents brought their children to Jesus for him to lay hands on them
and bless them, the disciples told them off. Jesus had quite different ideas
and proceeded to lay hands on them and bless them.

*Jesus said, "Let the little children come to me, and do not
hinder them, for the kingdom of heaven belongs to such as
these."*

Matthew 19:14

*Clearly this was a case of a child taken at random without
reference to the parents' faith and used as an example of the*

14

extent of grace. In the light of such scriptures it is difficult to conclude other than that children generally are under grace.

Rev. Colin Le Noury[4]

The Bride of Christ

God's eternal covenant relationship with Israel is portrayed as a marital relationship, with Israel being referred to as the unfaithful wife of God. In the book of Hosea, his wife Gomer's adulterous marital relationship is compared to Israel's relationship with the Lord:

...like an adulterous wife, this land is guilty of unfaithfulness to the LORD.

Hosea 1:2

When Jesus fulfilled all the Old Testament prophecies and came as the promised Messiah he made a new covenant with Israel.

"This is the covenant I will make with the people of Israel
after that time," declares the LORD.
"I will put my law in their minds
and write it on their hearts.
I will be their God,
and they will be my people."

Jeremiah 31:33

At the Passover supper with his disciples Jesus gave thanks and broke bread.

In the same way, after the supper he took the cup, saying, "This cup is the new covenant in my blood, which is poured out for you."

Luke 22:20

Believers are the bride of Christ and He is the bridegroom. This metaphor describes His relationship with his dearly beloved bride, the church. He reveals himself as a loving, faithful bridegroom who is committed to a covenant relationship with everyone who willingly accepts Him as their personal saviour and who willingly submits to His Lordship and authority.

---

[4] *Burning Questions 9;* Prophetic Witness Movement International

Our understanding of the Rapture is enhanced when we understand how a Galilean wedding is arranged. In Galilee, marriages were pre-arranged. The father of the bride would select a suitable bride (*kallah* in Hebrew) for his son, and a marriage covenant would be arranged.

No arrangements could proceed until the bride had willingly consented to the wedding. The bridegroom would set out in the legal agreement of betrothal his obligations, in a similar way that God has set out his promises to the church, his bride.

> *"I will betroth you in righteousness and justice,*
> *in love and compassion.*
> *I will betroth you in faithfulness,*
> *and you will acknowledge the LORD."*
>
> *Hosea 2:19-20*

A dowry would be agreed which was paid for by the bridegroom to provide for the bride in the event of divorce or his premature death. Hosea paid Gomer's dowry with precious coins: "So I bought her for myself for fifteen pieces of silver and a homer and a half of barley (the price of a common slave)." (Hos.3:2, AMP) Jacob paid Rachel's dowry with faithful service "in return for another seven years of work" (Gen.29:27). Our fallen nature meant the price the bridegroom had to pay was His life blood. "You were bought at a price" (1.Co.6:20) and "with the precious blood of Christ" (1.Pet.1:19).

Next comes a spiritual cleansing called a *mikvah* which is when the bride and bridegroom bathe separately in a sunken pool before entering into a spiritual covenant. This ceremonial cleansing represents the sinful nature being washed away and our being born again and receiving the Holy Spirit.

> *Husbands, love your wives, just as Christ loved the church and*
> *gave himself up for her to make her holy, cleansing her by the*
> *washing with water through the word, and to present her to*
> *himself as a radiant church, without stain or wrinkle or any*
> *other blemish, but holy and blameless.*
>
> *Ephesians 5:25-27*

Unlike our Western culture, where a period of courting is followed by the couple deciding to become engaged, then setting a date to become married, the Galilean betrothal was a legally binding covenant contract arranged between the two fathers. This declared the couple were legally married, although the union was not consummated until the marriage supper took place, about a year later.

At the Last Supper Jesus said:

> *"I tell you, I will not drink from this fruit of the vine from now on until that day when I drink it new with you in my Father's kingdom."*
>
> *Matthew 26:29*

The disciples were familiar with the wedding terminology Jesus used. In the Galilean wedding the bridegroom, apart from offering his bride a ring and a gift, would invite his bride to drink wine from the same cup as he had done. This indicated her willingness to be married and sealed the spiritual covenant, called the 'betrothal', when the bridegroom would say, "I shall not drink from the fruit of the vine, until I drink it with you, in my father's house." At this point they legally became a married couple, although they would not live together until perhaps a year later.

The disciples began to understand that Jesus Christ, the bridegroom, would be leaving them, his bride, for a time and would be preparing a future home for them in heaven; but he promised to return.

> *"If I go and prepare a place for you, I will come back and take you to be with me that you also may be where I am."*
>
> *John 14:3*

The bride would keep herself pure, holy and set apart for her bridegroom. Like the bride, the church must not be allowed to contaminate and spoil its relationship with Jesus Christ. She must be solely concerned with devoting herself wholly to Him and not indulge in things that are contrary to the word of God.

> *"You have been set apart as holy to the LORD your God, and he has chosen you from all the nations of the earth to be his own special treasure."*
>
> *Deuteronomy 14:2 (NLT)*

During the waiting period called the 'erusin period', the bridegroom would build an additional room at his father's house where they would live and the bride would make her wedding dress and those of her bridesmaids. She needed to be ready at a moment's notice for the unexpected but long-hoped-for arrival of the bridegroom.

When the disciples asked Jesus when he would return he told them:

"But about that day or hour no one knows, not even the angels in heaven, nor the Son, but only the Father."

Matthew 24:36

The disciples understood his meaning because in a Galilean wedding neither the bridegroom nor bride would know when the wedding celebrations would occur. It was only the bridegroom's father who could decide the date and time. This would happen during the hours of darkness and only when he was completely satisfied everything was ready. Jesus told his disciples they should always be prepared:

"Understand this: If the owner of the house had known at what time of night the thief was coming, he would have kept watch and would not have let his house be broken into."

Matthew 24:43

The bridegroom's father would inform his son the wedding could proceed and great excitement would occur when the *shofar* horn was loudly blown. This would wake up the guests and alert the bride and bridesmaids that the bridegroom was on his way. The similarities with the "trumpet call of God" (1.Thess.4:16) announcing the Rapture are striking.

Once the bridesmaids heard the *shofar* horn they checked their lamps for sufficient oil and helped the bride to get ready and put on her best wedding gown. The bride would be lifted up in a chair and carried, while the bridesmaids would escort her safely through the dark, to the bridegroom's father's house. The disciples appreciated the 'Parable of the Ten Virgins' who went out with their lamps to meet the bridegroom, as it portrayed a Galilean wedding, and would have understood the implications of not being ready.

"Five of them were foolish and five were wise. The foolish ones took their lamps but did not take any oil with them. The wise ones, however, took oil in jars along with their lamps. The bridegroom was a long time in coming, and they all became drowsy and fell asleep. At midnight the cry rang out: 'Here's the bridegroom! Come out to meet him!' Then all the virgins woke up and trimmed their lamps. The foolish ones said to the wise, 'Give us some of your oil; our lamps are going out.' 'No,' they replied, 'there may not be enough for both us and you. Instead, go to those who sell oil and buy some for

yourselves.' But while they were on their way to buy the oil, the bridegroom arrived. The virgins who were ready went in with him to the wedding banquet. And the door was shut."

Matthew 25:2-10

Once the wedding door was shut for the wedding banquet any latecomers would literally be shut out and not allowed in for the week-long banquet. Jesus made it clear to his disciples they must be prepared and ready for his unexpected return.

"Therefore keep watch, because you do not know the day or the hour."

Matthew 25:13

Jesus has promised to return for His bride, the church and take her to heaven where he is preparing a place for her.

"Do not let your hearts be troubled. You believe in God; believe also in me. My Father's house has many rooms; if that were not so, would I have told you that I am going there to prepare a place for you? And if I go and prepare a place for you, I will come back and take you to be with me that you also may be where I am."

John 14:1-3

Believers have been given plenty of time to prepare for the return of Jesus Christ. The fulfilment of prophecies are casting their shadow (see Matt.24) and we should be prepared for the imminency of our Bridegroom's return and be ready to leave.

Once the bride would arrive at the bridegroom's father's house, the wedding banquet would get underway. The meaning is clear: believers will be caught up at the Rapture to meet Jesus Christ when he returns and "we will be with the Lord forever" (1.Thess.4:17).

The Galilean celebrations will pale into insignificance in comparison with the joyful celebrations believers will enjoy when the Lord comes to rapture all those who love Him.

"Blessed are those who are invited to the wedding supper of the Lamb!"

Revelation 19:9

Rewards for Believers

Christians can look forward to rewards when they are raptured and arrive in heaven They will appear before the "judgment seat of Christ" (2.Cor.5:10), otherwise known as the 'bema seat'. The believer's judgement is not about salvation, for that is secure and settled, but it does concern how we have lived our lives since becoming a Christian and whether we have accomplished any worthwhile acts of service for Jesus Christ as faithful disciples.

> *For no one can lay any foundation other than the one already laid, which is Jesus Christ. If anyone builds on this foundation using gold, silver, costly stones, wood, hay or straw, their work will be shown for what it is, because the Day will bring it to light. It will be revealed with fire, and the fire will test the quality of each person's work. If what has been built survives, the builder will receive a reward. If it is burned up, the builder will suffer loss but yet will be saved – even though only as one escaping through the flames.*
>
> *1 Corinthians 3:11-15*

Unlike salvation, which is a free gift of grace, heavenly rewards are conditional on continued faithful service.

> *So then, each of us will give an account of ourselves to God.*
>
> *Romans 14:12*

This is when most believers will receive rewards and crowns for good works and faithful service.

> *For what is our hope, our joy, or the crown in which we will glory in the presence of our Lord Jesus when he comes? Is it not you? Indeed, you are our glory and joy.*
>
> *1 Thessalonians 2:19-20*

Many different kinds of rewards are promised for believers who have demonstrated faithfulness and performed works of service to others. There are also five crowns identified for a number of specific achievements that have been recorded in scripture:

- The 'crown of life' (also known as the 'martyr's crown') is awarded to those who are faithful despite suffering extreme persecution (see Jas.1:12).

- The 'victor's crown' (also known as the 'incorruptible crown for discipleship') is awarded for evangelism and faithful discipleship (see Rev.2:10).
- The 'crown of rejoicing' (also known as the 'soul-winner's crown') is awarded for evangelism and faithfully witnessing (see 1.Thess.2:19).
- The 'crown of glory' is awarded to faithful pastors and ministers who lead and serve wisely those in the church (see 1.Pet.5:2-4).
- The 'crown of righteousness' is awarded to those who are looking forward to, and joyfully preparing for, the return of Jesus Christ (see 2.Tim.4:7-8).

Prepare for the Rapture

While we wait for the return of Jesus Christ we are told to:

- be patient;

Be patient, then, brothers and sisters, until the Lord's coming. See how the farmer waits for the land to yield its valuable crop, patiently waiting for autumn and spring rains. You too, be patient and stand firm, because the Lord's coming is near.

James 5:7-8

- be alert;

Therefore, with minds that are alert and fully sober, set your hope on the grace to be brought to you when Jesus Christ is revealed at his coming.

1 Peter 1:13

- be obedient;

I charge you to keep this command without spot or blame until the appearing of our Lord Jesus Christ, which God will bring about in his own time – God, the blessed and only Ruler, the King of kings and Lord of lords.

1 Timothy 6:13-15

- be godly;

It teaches us to say 'No' to ungodliness and worldly passions, and to live self-controlled, upright and godly lives in this present age, while we wait for the blessed hope – the appearing of the glory of our great God and Savior, Jesus Christ.

Titus 2:12-13

- be holy.

May God himself, the God of peace, sanctify you through and through. May your whole spirit, soul and body be kept blameless at the coming of our Lord Jesus Christ.

1 Thessalonians 5:23

Events Following the Rapture

THE GREAT TRIBULATION

Following the Rapture the Lord Jesus Christ will remove the 'restrainer' from the world, which is God's presence, his Holy Spirit, which indwells believers, who are his ambassadors in the world. The judgement of God, known as the Tribulation, will follow and last for a period of seven years. The Antichrist will be revealed when he signs a seven-year covenant (*hephtod* in Hebrew) between the nation of Israel and the world. This will inaugurate the Tribulation period, a time when God allows Satan to rule unhindered on earth. After 42 months the Antichrist will break this seven-year covenant with Israel and reveal his true intentions by desecrating the rebuilt holy temple and announcing that he is God. He will require everybody to worship him and those who refuse to do so will be killed.

"He will confirm a covenant with many for one 'seven'. In the middle of the 'seven' he will put an end to sacrifice and offering. And at the temple he will set up an abomination that causes desolation, until the end that is decreed is poured out on him."

Daniel 9:27

This will be a time of great suffering for unbelievers but they will be given further opportunities to repent and be saved from God's wrath. During the first 42 months of the Tribulation, Jesus Christ "will appoint [His] two witnesses, and they will prophesy for 1,260 days, clothed in sackcloth" (Rev.11:3). Many people will turn to Christ and be saved although it will be at a great cost to themselves. The Tribulation will end with the Battle of Armageddon, at which time Jesus Christ's heavenly army will crush the Antichrist and False Prophet in a short-lived battle.

And I saw an angel coming down out of heaven, having the key to the Abyss and holding in his hand a great chain. He seized the dragon, that ancient serpent, who is the devil, or Satan, and bound him for a thousand years. He threw him into the Abyss, and locked and sealed it over him, to keep him from deceiving the nations anymore until the thousand years were ended.

Revelation 20:1-3

THE SECOND COMING OF JESUS CHRIST

This will herald the most spectacular event in the history of the world, the Second Coming of Jesus Christ'(the Greek word *parousia* means 'a coming').

"People will faint from terror, apprehensive of what is coming on the world, for the heavenly bodies will be shaken. At that time they will see the Son of Man coming in a cloud with power and great glory."

Luke 21:26-27

At his Second Coming, Jesus Christ will touch down on the Mount of Olives causing it to "split in two from east to west, forming a great valley with half of the mountain moving north and half moving south" (Zech.14:4).

"Immediately after the distress of those days the sun will be darkened, and the moon will not give its light; the stars will fall from the sky, and the heavenly bodies will be shaken."

Matthew 24:29

This momentous event will be unlike anything that has ever happened in the history of the world. At the Rapture the believers silently and instantly rise to meet the Lord in the air, but at the Second Coming of Jesus Christ the believers accompany Jesus Christ as he returns to earth to judge the nations and the unbelievers of the world.

See, the Lord is coming with thousands upon thousands of his holy ones to judge everyone, and to convict all of them of all the ungodly acts they have committed in their ungodliness, and of all the defiant words ungodly sinners have spoken against him.

Jude 14-15

At the Rapture, only the believers will see Jesus Christ, but at His Second Coming everyone in the world will witness this event, possibly through the medium of TV or the Internet. This time the Jews will realise that the Messiah came two thousand years before but they didn't recognise him and had him crucified on a cross. At the Second Coming of Jesus Christ, the Jews will realise their mistake and be filled with regret and great sadness.

"Look, he is coming with the clouds,"
and "every eye will see him,
even those who pierced him;"
and all peoples on earth "will mourn because of him."
So shall it be! Amen.

Revelation 1:7

THE MILLENNIAL REIGN OF JESUS CHRIST

When Jesus Christ returns with all believers, it will be to rule the world for a thousand years, an event known as the Millennial Reign of Jesus Christ. This is when the world will experience the perfection of divine rule.

Blessed and holy are those who share in the first resurrection.
The second death has no power over them, but they will be
priests of God and of Christ and will reign with him for a
thousand years.

Revelation 20:6

THE DAY OF JUDGEMENT

Just as people are destined to die once, and after that to face judgement, so Christ was sacrificed once to take away the sins of many; and he will appear a second time, not to bear sin, but to bring salvation to those who are waiting for him.

Hebrews 9:27-28

The Millennium will conclude with Satan's destruction and the Day of Judgement for unbelievers who will appear before the "great white throne" (Rev.20:11) to face Almighty God. Unless their names appear in the "book of life" (Rev.20:15) they will be condemned to the "lake of fire" (Rev.20:14) for their unbelief.

They will be punished with everlasting destruction and shut out from the presence of the Lord and from the glory of his might on the day he comes to be glorified in his holy people and to be marveled at among all those who have believed.

2 Thessalonians 1:9-10

THE NEW HEAVEN AND NEW EARTH

The apostle Paul tells us:

Our citizenship is in heaven and we eagerly await a Savior from there, the Lord Jesus Christ, who by the power that enables him to bring everything under his control, will transform our lowly bodies so that they will be like his heavenly body.

Philippians 3:20-21

Jesus Christ will set up his perfect kingdom on earth where he will rule from the holy city of Jerusalem with believers. We are given a foretaste of our ultimate eternal future in the final two chapters of the Bible (Rev.21-22) where we learn all believers will live with God and be able to have fellowship directly with Him.

Then I saw "a new heaven and a new earth," for the first heaven and the first earth had passed away, and there was no longer any sea. I saw the Holy City, the new Jerusalem, coming down out of heaven from God, prepared as a bride beautifully dressed for her husband. And I heard a loud voice from the throne saying, "Look! God's dwelling place is now among the people, and he will dwell with them. They will be his people, and God himself will be with them and be their God. 'He will wipe away every tear from their eyes. There will be no more death' or mourning or crying or pain, for the old order of things has passed away."

Revelation 21:1-4

25

Points for Reflection

- It is an inescapable fact of life that all people are destined to die, but, "I tell you, now is the time of God's favor, now is the day of salvation." (2.Cor.6:2)

- Many believers will still be alive when the Rapture of the Church takes place and anyone who is not born again will be left behind. Those left behind will experience the Great Tribulation with all its suffering and horrors, which hopefully will persuade many to repent and be saved from eternity in the lake of fire.

- In the next chapter we examine what the Tribulation will entail for those who reject the free gift of salvation through Jesus Christ. After the Rapture of the Church there will be utter chaos throughout the world, as all those who have been born again are suddenly and without warning snatched from the earth. Once this occurs the wrath of God will be poured out on unbelievers throughout the world.

- First of all Jesus Christ will open the 'seven seals' in sequential order, followed by the 'seven trumpet' judgements. This will occur during the first half of the period of Tribulation (three and a half years). After the angels pour out the 'seven bowls' of judgement in the second half of the Great Tribulation, the world as we know it will be changed beyond all recognition by the devastation that will follow. These extraordinary events which precede the Second Coming of Jesus Christ are examined in Chapter 2.

Questions

"The Spirit clearly says that in later times some will abandon the faith and follow deceiving spirits and things taught by demons." (1.Tim.4:1) Is there clear evidence this is happening in the 21st century?

_____

_____

During the last war (1939-1945) many people thought the Rapture of the Church would be very soon. "You will hear of wars and rumors of wars but see to it you are not alarmed." (Matt.24:6) Does this mean there are more serious wars to come?

_____

What does the difference between the Rapture and the Second Coming of Jesus Christ mean for believers?

_____

_____

How does the Galilean wedding help our understanding of the Rapture?

_____

_____

Where do we learn in scripture that children below the age of responsibility and accountability will be raptured?

_____

_____

When will it be too late for an unbeliever to repent and receive the free gift of salvation?

_____

_____

CHAPTER TWO

The Great Tribulation (I)

Introduction

The Greek word for tribulation *(thlipsis)* means 'to crush or press together'. It is a strong term which is used to refer to real hardship and occurs forty-five times in the New Testament. Once the Rapture takes place, soon after a period the Bible describes as "great tribulation" (Rev.7:14) will commence. This time of Tribulation is also referred to as the great day of God's wrath.

> *"For the great day of their wrath has come and who can withstand it?"*
>
> *Revelation 6:17*

What is the Great Tribulation?

Those left behind after the Rapture will be subject to totalitarian rule by a man known as the Antichrist but described in the Bible as "the beast" (Rev.13:18 – *ghrion* in the Greek). This seven-year period of Tribulation begins with the Antichrist signing a covenant (a legally binding peace treaty) with Israel, which he breaks after 1,260 days (Dan.9:27) revealing his true character and wickedness. Once the Antichrist takes power, his autocratic, tyrannical 'One World Government' will take control of the monetary system, all economic activity, and curtail individual freedom. When he breaks the peace treaty with Israel, he will desecrate the temple and declare that he is God and demand everyone worships him alone. Interestingly, the $1 bill, originally issued in 1862 during the American civil war, contains on the back the Latin inscription *'Novus Ordo Seclorum'* which means 'New Order of the Ages'.

The False Prophet, known as the second beast, operates with the delegated authority of the first beast to form a 'One World Religion'.

It exercised all the authority of the first beast on its behalf and made the earth and its inhabitants worship the first beast whose fatal wound had been healed.

Revelation 13:12

Everyone who refuses to worship the image of the Antichrist will be killed (see Rev.13:15).

It also forced all people great and small, rich and poor, free and slave, to receive a mark on their right hands or on their foreheads, so that they could not buy or sell unless they had the mark, which is the name of the beast or the number of its name.

Revelation 13:16-17

The "mark" or *charagma* in Greek, means 'a tattoo'. The biblical reference suggests the mark will be *on* people, not *in* them.

Notice that this mark will be on people, not in them (like some kind of microchip). It will be on the right hand or forehead and will be visible to the eye (perhaps like a tattoo,) not hidden beneath the skin.

Ron Rhodes[5]

The reference to the beast and the Antichrist are one and the same.

Let the person who has insight calculate the number of the beast, for it is the number of a man. That number is 666.

Revelation 13:18

Those refusing to accept the mark of the beast will be unable to rent or purchase a home, pay any bills, or shop for food and necessities. Any withdrawal of savings or investments will be prohibited, so the victims will suffer great hardship and many will die of disease or malnutrition. The technology for controlling economic activity is available today and could easily be implemented in our society. Every financial transaction would be capable of being monitored were an electronic cashless society to become mandatory, with biometric identification available using hand, retina and facial recognition scanners and CCTV.

The Bible warns everyone not to worship the beast, or to take the mark of the beast, the Antichrist. Everyone who rejects God and chooses

---

[5] *Unmasking the Antichrist;* p.174

to serve Satan during the coming Tribulation must be prepared to live with the irreversible consequences and will incur God's wrath. This is why it is so important that unbelievers repent now and become followers of Jesus Christ before the time of Tribulation.

> *"If anyone worships the beast and its image and receives its mark on their forehead or on their hand, they, too, will drink the wine of God's fury, which has been poured full strength into the cup of his wrath."*
>
> Revelation 14:9-10

The Bible warns that those who repent and become believers during this time will probably become martyrs.

> *Then I heard a voice from heaven say, "Write this: Blessed are the dead who die in the Lord from now on."*
>
> Revelation 14:13

The Antichrist will not tolerate anyone who does not worship him; they will be put to death.

The book of Revelation describes in chapters 6-16 how God will unleash his wrath on unbelievers during this time of Tribulation. Life on earth will quickly becoming intolerable following the Rapture of the Church.

> *"There will be a time of distress such as has not happened from the beginning of nations until then. But at that time your people – everyone whose name is found written in the book – will be delivered."*
>
> Daniel 12:1

God will start to vent his fury on this chaotic, decadent world when Jesus Christ "the Lamb" (Rev.6:1) opens the first seal. The Greek word *sphragis* means 'seal'.[6]

> *Don't you know that you yourselves are God's temple and that God's spirit dwells in your midst?*
>
> 1 Corinthians 3:16

The Holy Spirit is more powerful than Satan "because the one who is in you is greater than the one who is in the world".

---

[6] *Strong's Exhaustive Concordance of the Bible*

The time of Tribulation will commence after the Rapture of the Church and over time the severity of tribulation will grow in intensity. The cumulative effect of opening first the seals, then the trumpets and finally, in the second half of the Tribulation, the bowls, will be horrific and intense.

Life Under Tribulation: The Seven Seals

Before Jesus Christ opens the first seal the world will still be in a high state of turmoil because millions of Christians and all children will have disappeared from the world. No health and public services will function properly; law and order will break down; commerce, business, banking and travel arrangements will be in a state of disarray; and severe inflation caused by shortages will overwhelm the world. Those bent on causing mayhem will thrive under the Antichrist's regime: terrorists, anarchists and criminal gangs will flourish; looting will be commonplace as people struggle to provide the necessities of life for themselves.

I watched as the Lamb opened the first of the seven seals.

Revelation 6:1

The <u>first four</u> seals loosen the constraints on Satan and the four horsemen of the apocalypse ride out to unleash violence, war, famine and death.

I looked and there before me was a <u>white</u> horse! Its rider held a bow, and he was given a crown, and he rode out as a conqueror bent on conquest.

Revelation 6:2 (underlining added)

The crown suggests that this individual is a ruler. The bow without an arrow, may indicate symbolically that the antichrist will initially establish his world government without warfare.

Ron Rhodes[7]

A horseman who "rode out as a conqueror bent on conquest" describes a successful national leader with a reputation for winning battles and who intends to invade other countries in the quest for more power, influence and territory.

---

[7] *Unmasking the Antichrist;* p.174

Ancient readers would have readily understood that this horseman meant conquest and war.

Craig S. Keener[8]

The second horse is <u>fiery red</u>. "Its rider was given the power to takes peace from the earth." (Rev.6:4a) He will prevent peaceful solutions being negotiated and ensure violence is used to settle disputes. He will permit vigilante justice and "make people kill each another" (Rev.6:4b).

The third horseman rides a <u>black</u> horse. "Its rider was holding a pair of scales in his hand." (Rev.6:5) This horseman causes severe famine by disrupting economic activity, contriving wars, promoting anarchy and general lawlessness. This will result in hyperinflation and ordinary households will find they are only able to buy "two pounds of wheat for a day's wages and six pounds of barley for a day's wages" (Rev.6:6).

A person with average earnings of £25,000 per annum, would find that a small loaf of bread weighing about 2 lbs (costing a little over £1 today) would cost about £100. Most families would be on starvation rations and many people will resort to looting shops and businesses in order to survive.

Once the fourth seal is opened, John's attention is drawn to a <u>pale green</u> horse.

Its rider was named Death, and Hades was following close behind him. They were given power over a fourth of the earth to kill by sword, famine and plague, and by the wild beasts of the earth.

Revelation 6:8

Many lives will be endangered as a result of famine coupled with widespread lawlessness. Poor families and elderly persons on social security benefits will suffer malnutrition and many will die. Others may resort to prostitution in order to make ends meet. Widespread looting will make families feel unsafe even in their own homes. The fate of those in hospitals, care homes and those with special needs, may be decided by mob rule. A population desperate for food might introduce compulsory euthanasia to ensure the survival of the fittest. Fear for the individual's safety would be widespread and people will despair as marauding

---

[8] *The Bible Background Commentary;* p.780

criminal gangs plunder people's homes, attack individuals and kill vulnerable persons with impunity.

In addition to the disasters already unleashed, the power to kill by plague may involve the use of deadly bacteria, viruses and pandemics like the coronavirus Covid-19 to spread fatal disease. During the bubonic plague or 'Black Death' in 1346, people were covered in black boils, oozed blood and pus, and the plague resulted in the deaths of over 20 million people. Later, in the 'Great Plague' of 1665, a quarter of London's population died in the space of eighteen months by 'Yersinia pestis bacterium', a plague transmitted through the bite of infected rat fleas.

When the <u>fifth</u> seal is opened, the apostle John "saw under the altar the souls of those who had been slain because of the word of God and the testimony they had maintained" (Rev.6:9). The Antichrist will vent his fury against anyone who becomes a believer, and those who become martyrs appeal to God for justice and retribution. The martyred believers are given a white robe but "they were told to wait a little longer until the full number of their fellow servants, their brothers and sisters, were killed just as they had been" (Rev.6:11). They are told to be patient because God in his mercy is allowing more time for unbelievers to repent, and the total number of those who will become martyrs during the Tribulation has not been reached.

The opening of the <u>sixth</u> seal unleashes a colossal earthquake which is likely to precipitate extensive tsunamis. Unprecedented cosmic disturbances take place, including the sun turning black, the moon turning red and other terrifying signs in the sky.

> *I watched as he opened the sixth seal. There was a great earthquake. The sun turned black like sackcloth made of goat hair, the whole moon turned blood red, and the stars in the sky fell to earth, as figs drop from a fig-tree when shaken by a strong wind. The heavens receded like a scroll being rolled up, and every mountain and island was removed from its place.*
>
> *Revelation 6:12-14*

Falling stars (or shooting stars) are streaks of light sometimes seen in the night sky caused by tiny bits of dust and rock called meteoroids, that fall into the earth's atmosphere and burn up. If a meteoroid hits the earth it will cause shockwaves and craters; but should a large one strike the ocean, it will cause earthquakes and tsunamis.

In 1908 a meteor 200 feet wide hit Siberia, causing devastation over an area of 1,000 square miles and uprooted trees up to 20 miles away. In the Old Testament powerful earthquakes were associated with the end of the age, and large earthquakes caused devastation in first century Asia Minor.[9]

> *You will flee as you fled from the earthquake in the days of Uzziah king of Judah.*
>
> Zechariah 14:5

> *"The fish in the sea, the birds in the sky, the beasts of the field, every creature that moves along the ground, and all the people on the face of the earth will tremble at my presence. The mountains will be overturned, the cliffs will crumble, and every wall will fall to the ground."*
>
> Ezekiel 38:20

Darkness and cosmic disturbances were seen as another sign of coming judgement.

> *"When I snuff you out, I will cover the heavens and darken their stars; I will cover the sun with a cloud, and the moon will not give its light."*
>
> Ezekiel 32:7

> *"The sun will be turned to darkness and the moon to blood before the coming of the great and dreadful day of the LORD."*
>
> Joel 2:31

Other frightening events, completely unprecedented in the history of the earth, will occur as each mountain and island is "removed from its place" (Rev.6:14). When the mountains start to break apart and huge rocks are falling, this will engender so much undiluted terror, everyone will want the rocks to fall on them and put them out of their misery.

---

[9] See Craig S. Keener; *The Bible Background Commentary*

*Then the kings of the earth, the princes, the generals, the rich,
the mighty, and everyone else, both slave and free, hid in caves
and among the rocks of the mountains.*

Revelation 6:15

The human race will have no response to these terrifying events.
Politicians and generals with their huge arsenals of nuclear weapons,
artillery and other weaponry will have no idea what to do. Everyone will
take to the only safe places on earth – the caves and underground bunkers
– like rats in a sewer. They will have no dignity but act out of fear and
the survival instinct.

These cataclysmic events will make everyone realise that these
disasters have been caused by the Creator of the universe and they are at
the complete mercy of Almighty God. But, rather than cry out to God in
repentance and seek His forgiveness, they call out to the mountains and
the rocks instead.

*"Fall on us and hide us from the face of him who sits on the
throne and from the wrath of the Lamb!"*

Revelation 6:16

The 144,000 Jewish Evangelists

After the cataclysmic earthquake that follows the opening of the sixth
seal, the realization dawns on everybody that the wrath of God and Jesus
Christ has been let loose.

*"...the great day of their wrath has come, and who can
withstand it?"*

Revelation 6:17

*After this I saw four angels standing at the four corners of the
earth, holding back the four winds of the earth to prevent any
wind from blowing on the land or the sea or on any tree.*

Revelation 7:1

The four winds blowing together from the north, south, east and west
mean dreadful and widespread destruction is foretold. The winds are held
back in order for the 144,000 "servants of our God" to have a seal placed
on their forehead, which was a sign of God's ownership and protection.

*Then I saw another angel coming up from the east, having the
seal of the living God. He called out in a loud voice to the four*

angels who had been given power to harm the land and the sea: "Do not harm the land or the sea or the trees until we put a seal on the foreheads of the servants of our God." Then I heard the number of those who were sealed: 144,000 from all the tribes of Israel.

Revelation 7:2-4

There were 12,000 from the tribes of Judah, Reuben, Gad, Asher, Naphtali Manasseh, Simeon, Levi, Issachar, Zebulun, Joseph and the tribe of Benjamin (see Rev.7:5-8). The tribe of Dan was not included and had been replaced by the tribe of Manasseh instead. This is because the tribe of Dan were unfaithful and King Jeroboam made two golden calves for the people to worship; one he placed in Bethel the other he set up in Dan (see 1.Kgs.12:28-29). The tribe of Dan will be included in the Millennium: "Dan will have one portion."(Ez.48:1)

During this pause in end time events, we learn God has selected a special group of 144,000 Jews to preach the gospel of the Kingdom, during the first half of the Tribulation. Things are about to get much worse, but God is allowing a final chance for unbelievers to be saved.

Instead he is patient with you, not wanting anyone to perish, but everyone to come to repentance.

2 Peter 3:9

This outpouring of the Holy Spirit will take place before an image of the Antichrist is set up in the temple declaring he is God and forcing everyone to worship him.

"I will pour out my Spirit in those days.
I will show wonders in the heavens
and on the earth,
blood and fire and billows of smoke.
The sun will be turned to darkness
and the moon to blood
before the coming of the great and dreadful day of the
LORD.
And everyone who calls
on the name of the LORD will be saved;
for on Mount Zion and in Jerusalem
there will be deliverance,
as the LORD has said,

even among the survivors
whom the LORD calls."

Joel 2:30-32

The next sight John witnesses is incredible. An enormous number have responded to the gospel message from the "servants of God" and have assembled before the throne of God wearing white robes signifying their righteousness and holding palm branches in their hands.

I looked and there before me was a great multitude that no one could count from every nation, tribe, people and language, standing before the throne and before the Lamb.

Revelation 7:9

Tim LaHaye believes this verse "indicates that during the first part of the Tribulation the greatest soul harvest in all history will take place"[10].

The presence of the 144,000 "before the throne of God" indicates that they are not on the earth but have already died and are serving the Lord "day and night in his temple" (Rev.7:15). These saints are singing, "Salvation belongs to our God, who sits on the throne, and to the Lamb," (Rev.7:10) which confirms they are saved and are celebrating their salvation.

"These are they that have come out of the great tribulation; they have washed their robes and made them white in the blood of the Lamb."

Revelation 7:14

They have endured "great tribulation" and suffered enormously, but have been promised that they will never have to endure any further suffering.

"For the Lamb at the center of the throne
will be their shepherd;
'he will lead them to springs of living water.'
'And God will wipe away every tear from their eyes.'"

Revelation 7:17

---

[10] *Revelation Unveiled;* p.153

CHAPTER THREE

The Great Tribulation (II)

Introduction

When he opened the seventh seal, there was silence in heaven for about half an hour.

Revelation 8:1

During this silence an angel presents the prayers of all believers to God in the form of incense in a "censer", which would be offered on the golden altar by a priest in the earthly temple.

Then the angel took the censer, filled it with fire from the altar, and hurled it on the earth; and there came peals of thunder, rumblings, flashes of lightning and an earthquake.

Revelation 8:5

The Seven Trumpets

Once the <u>first</u> trumpet sounded...

...there came hail, and fire mixed with blood, and it was hurled down on the earth. A third of the earth was burned up, a third of the trees were burned up, and all the green grass was burned up.

Revelation 8:7

In *Unmasking the Antichrist*, Ron Rhodes points out "that there may be nuclear detonations in the end times"[11]. This unprecedented destruction of one third of the earth, trees and grass in the world coupled with the painful "ugly festering sores [which] broke out on the people" (Rev.16:2) could be the result of radiation poisoning following the detonation of nuclear weapons.

---

[11] Ron Rhodes; *Unmasking the Antichrist;* p.205

"People will faint from terror, apprehensive of what is coming on the world, for the heavenly bodies will be shaken."

Luke 21:26

He concludes that "technology clearly now exists to burn a third of the earth and cause mass casualties".

This scorching of the earth will have a devastating effect on the environment and the capability of the world to farm the land, feed the cattle and provide enough food to feed the population of the world. According to the National Geographic Society, trees cover about 30% of the world's land mass and 250 million people live in the forests together with 80% of animals, plants and many species of birds. The destruction of a third of the trees and grassland by fire would result in wildfires covering the towns and cities in a dark haze and release huge amounts of carbon dioxide causing extreme temperature changes.

When the <u>second</u> trumpet is sounded…

> *…something like a huge mountain, all ablaze, was thrown into the sea. A third of the sea turned into blood, a third of the living creatures in the sea died, and a third of the ships were destroyed.*

Revelation 8:9

This description is compatible with an asteroid hitting an ocean as it is "something like a huge mountain" hurtling through space. Scientists believe if an asteroid were to hit the earth's atmosphere it would burn, causing a tremendous earthquake and tsunamis, and bringing widespread devastation to the world. Asteroids are masses of rock which vary in size from a few miles to hundreds of miles across. Scientists at NASA have charted over one million asteroids circling the sun which are larger than one kilometre in diameter, and millions of smaller ones.[12] The largest are Ceres, 620 miles in diameter; Pallas, 320 miles in diameter; and Vesta, 240 miles in diameter. Even a small asteroid hitting the sea would cause tsunamis that would wreak devastation for hundreds of miles.

The effect of an asteroid strike would be immense. When scientists completed the first global census of marine life in 2010, they identified 230,000 different kinds of marine life in the oceans, of which 22,000 species were fish. They estimated the number of fish in the oceans was

---

[12] Source: NASA Science: Solar System Exploration

three and a half trillion (3,500,000,000,000).[13] Using the results of this census and the biblical account that one third of marine life will die and one third of the world's shipping fleets will sink, the impact would be unimaginable.

> *Whatever the burning mountain is, it kills a third of the ocean life and destroys a third of the sea vessels. There has never been such a singular catastrophic event recorded of this magnitude in the history of humanity.*
>
> Tim LaHaye & Ed Hindson[14]

The sinking of one third of the world's merchant shipping, which currently amounts to 53,732 ships, would be an economic catastrophe. It would mean in the region of 17,900 merchant ships, including 3,850 bulk carriers, 5,650 cargo ships, 1,720 container ships and 2,840 oil tankers with their cargos totalling one million tons would sink simultaneously. Additionally, if a third of the 314 cruise ships, with a maximum capacity of 537,000 passengers, were to sink, it would be an enormous death toll.[15]

> *The third angel sounded his trumpet, and a great star, blazing like a torch, fell from the sky on a third of the rivers and on the springs of water – the name of the star is Wormwood. A third of the waters turned bitter, and many people died from the waters that had become bitter.*
>
> Revelation 8:10-11 (underlining added)

This deadly contamination of the earth's water supplies will lead to a swift death by dehydration and destroy irrigation and fishing resources. A prominent Russia atheist writer pointed out the apocalyptic falling star named "Wormwood" was the same word used to describe a bitter wild herb used as a tonic in Russia. The Ukrainian word for "Wormwood" is Chernobyl.[16] As if the colossal disturbances made to the environment coupled with worldwide economic ruin were not enough for mankind to endure, there is now the overpowering stink of one trillion

---

[13] *The Census of Marine Life: 'Making Ocean Life Count'*
[14] *The Popular Bible Prophecy Commentary;* p.518
[15] Cruise Market Watch; 2018
[16] *New York Times;* 26 July 1986

(1,000,000,000,000) rotting fish on the seashore, choking smoke everywhere and people staggering around dying from dehydration.

Once the <u>fourth</u> trumpet sounds one third of the sun, moon and stars turn dark.

> *A third of the day was without light, and also a third of the night.*
>
> *Revelation 8:12*

This would make the earth much cooler and the impenetrable darkness will make travel and all activity more difficult and challenging. When Pharaoh refused to let the Israelites leave Egypt, God sent a plague of darkness on the Egyptians and Moses was told to…

> *"Stretch out your hand towards the sky so that darkness spreads over Egypt – darkness that can be felt."*
>
> *Exodus 10:21*

As the <u>fifth</u> angel sounds his trumpet, which is the <u>first woe</u>, a star falls from heaven and a trusted angelic being unlocks the Abyss. Tim LaHaye and Ed Hindson explain that, "Coming from heaven this angel would be one of the servants of the Lord and not an evil agent of Satan."[17] Once the Abyss is unlocked it releases so much smoke that it virtually blots out the light from the sun.

> *When he opened the Abyss, smoke rose from it like the smoke from a gigantic furnace. The sun and sky were darkened by the smoke from the Abyss. And out of the smoke locusts came down on the earth and were given power like that of scorpions of the earth.*
>
> *Revelation 9:2-3*

The locusts are told not to harm the trees, the plants or the 144,000 Jews who have God's seal on their foreheads; but everybody else would experience immense suffering.

> *They were not allowed to kill them but only to torture them for five months. And the agony they suffered was like that of the sting of a scorpion when it strikes.*
>
> *Revelation 9:5*

---

[17] Tim LaHaye & Ed Hindson; *The Popular Bible Prophecy Commentary*

These locusts are clearly demons so could not be destroyed by humans.

> *They had as king over them the angel of the Abyss, whose name in Hebrew is Abaddon and in Greek is Apollyon (that is, Destroyer).*
>
> *Revelation 9:11*

> *Most believe this is a fallen archangel who serves Satan, but some think this could be Satan himself. Whatever the case he is never connected directly with the abyss until he is finally cast into it at the very end of human history.*
>
> *Tim LaHaye & Ed Hindson[18]*

> *He threw him into the Abyss, and locked and sealed it over him.*
>
> *Revelation 20:1-3*

These demons have bodies like horses, their faces resemble those of men, they wear crowns of gold and have long hair, teeth like lions and wear breastplates made of iron. Their wings make a thunderous noise in flight and they have tails with stingers like scorpions. The pain from their sting is so agonising, the victims will want to die but cannot.

According to scientists, the sting from a scorpion is very painful because the stingers on the ends of their tails pierce the skin of the victims and inject venom. The venom is designed to cause so much pain, predators leave them alone. Researchers have discovered a scorpion's venom contains 100 toxins and the main pain-causing ingredient is a peptide called BmP01. This product is able to magnify the pain signals to the body due to the acidity of the venom.[19]

At the sounding of the <u>sixth</u> trumpet, which is the <u>second woe</u>, a voice from the golden altar before God commands the angel:

> *"Release the four angels who are bound at the great river Euphrates."*
>
> *Revelation 9:14*

---

[18] *The Popular Bible Prophecy Commentary*
[19] *Science Advances;* vol.3, no.8; 2 August 2017

These four captive angels being held at the River Euphrates are released to get ready to lead their massive army for the final battle of Armageddon.

The four angels bound in the Euphrates are fallen ones. Good angels are never bound. They are the leaders of the 200 million demon horsemen who are now bound in the abyss and who will be loosed under the sixth trumpet to cause the second woe announced by the angel.

Finis Jennings Dake[20]

The Euphrates is the longest and one of the most historically important rivers of Western Asia. Together with the Tigris, it is one of the two defining rivers of Mesopotamia (the 'Land between the Rivers'). Originating in the Armenian Highlands (Eastern Turkey), the Euphrates flows through Syria and Iraq to join the Tigris in the Shatt al-Arab, which empties into the Persian Gulf.[21]

So the four angels, who had been prepared for the (appointed) hour and day and month and year, were released to kill a third of mankind. The number of the troops of cavalry was twice ten thousand times ten thousand (two hundred million); I heard the number of them.

Revelation 9:16 (AMP)

The appearance of this massive army of demons is very frightening.

The riders had breastplates (the color) of fire and of hyacinth (sapphire blue) and of brimstone (yellow); and the heads of the horses looked like the heads of lions, and from out of their mouths came fire and smoke and brimstone (burning sulpur). A third of mankind was killed by these three plagues – by the fire and the smoke and the brimstone that came from the mouths of the horses.

Revelation 9:17b-18 (AMP)

Based on the current world population of 7.8 billion the number of humans who will die by the three plagues of fire, smoke and sulphur will be less than 2.6 billion (2,600,000,000) because the church and

---

[20] *Dake's Annotated Reference Bible*
[21] Source: Wikipedia

Tribulation martyrs will not be on earth when this occurs. Despite this colossal loss of life, the survivors will be unwilling to change their ungodly lifestyle and criminal behaviour and respond to the opportunity God is giving them, in his grace and mercy, to be saved.

> *The rest of mankind who were not killed by these plagues still did not repent of the work of their hands; they did not stop worshiping demons, and idols of gold, silver, bronze, stone and wood – idols that cannot see or hear or walk. Nor did they repent of their murders, their magic arts, their sexual immorality or their thefts.*
>
> *Revelation 9:20-21*

Before the seventh trumpet sounds, an almighty angel appears from heaven holding a little scroll. He gives a loud shout like the roar of a lion and the voices of the thunders speak.

> *I was about to write; but I heard a voice from heaven say, "Seal up what the seven thunders have said and do not write it down."*
>
> *Revelation 10:4*

This remains a mystery, but John is told, "You must prophesy again about many peoples, nations, languages and kings." (Rev.10:11)

Apparently, God's plan and outline for the last half of the Tribulation is in the little scroll and John is commanded that he "must prophesy" about what is on the horizon. The horrors of God's coming wrath give John heartburn and indigestion, but it also tastes good as honey because the final stages of God's plan include the coming of the Son of God's plan to bring peace to the earth.[22]

The Two Witnesses

The next important development concerns the two witnesses.

> *They are "the two olive trees" and the two lampstands, and "they stand before the Lord of the earth."*
>
> *Revelation 11:4*

---

[22] See Tim LaHaye & Ed Hindson; *The Popular Bible Prophecy Commentary;* p.521

This fulfils the prophecy of Zechariah:

> *"What are these two olive trees on the right and the left of the lampstand? ... These are the two who are anointed to serve the Lord of all the earth."*
>
> *Zechariah 4:12,14*

These two witnesses are dressed in sackcloth and they prophesy in the city for 1,260 days. Sackcloth was traditionally worn by those recently bereaved, but these two prophets are dressed in sackcloth as a sign of repentance. When Jonah warned the city of Ninevah that God would overthrow the city in forty days unless they repented of their wicked ways, they took his warning seriously and demonstrated their repentance by dressing in sackcloth.

> *The Ninevites believed God. A fast was proclaimed, and all of them, from the greatest to the least, put on sackcloth.*
>
> *Jonah 3:5*

When God saw that they had listened to his warnings, "he relented and did not bring on them the destruction he had threatened" (Jnh.3:10b).

The two prophets prophesy in Jerusalem throughout the first half of the Tribulation and are able to perform miracles, preach the gospel message of salvation and are empowered by the Holy Spirit to be witnesses for God.

> *If anyone tries to harm them, fire comes from their mouths and devours their enemies.*
>
> *Revelation 11:5*

They are given the power to inflict plagues on the earth, to "turn the waters into blood" (Rev.11: 6b) including withholding the rains causing drought, as in the days of Elijah:

> *"There will be neither dew nor rain in the next few years except at my word."*
>
> *1 Kings 17:1*

The identity of both witnesses has not been revealed, but the prophet Malachi discloses that Elijah the prophet will return before the "day of the Lord", which would be during the period of Tribulation. Elijah did not die naturally but "a chariot of fire and horses of fire appeared and

separated the two of them and Elijah went up to heaven in a whirlwind"
(2.Kgs.2:11).

> *So, before the Great Tribulation starts, Elijah will return,*
> *perhaps as one of the two witnesses.*
>
> Tim LaHaye & Ed Hindson[23]

Paul Yonggi Cho believes Moses and Elijah are the two witnesses who
will come and prophesy,[24] a view shared by Jeff Kinley.[25] When Peter,
James and John accompanied Jesus to the Mount of Transfiguration to
pray, Moses and Elijah appeared to them.

> *As he was praying, the appearance of his face changed, and*
> *his clothes became as bright as a flash of lightning. Two men,*
> *Moses and Elijah, appeared in glorious splendor, talking with*
> *Jesus. They spoke about his departure, which he was about to*
> *bring to fulfilment at Jerusalem. Peter and his companions*
> *were very sleepy, but when they became fully awake, they saw*
> *his glory and the two men standing with him.*
>
> Luke 9:29-31

When the two witnesses return to earth they will testify to the fact
that people receive salvation through faith in Jesus Christ who shed his
precious blood of the cross. They will testify and warn that the Antichrist
is not the Messiah but the son of perdition (*apoleia* in the Greek) and
finally they will warn of the imminent judgement of God.

> *"See, I will send you the prophet Elijah to you before that*
> *great and dreadful day of the LORD comes. He will turn the*
> *hearts of the parents to their children, and the hearts of the*
> *children to their parents; or else I will come and strike the land*
> *with total destruction."*
>
> Malachi 4:5-6

They will be filled with the Holy Spirit and exercise spiritual gifts,
perform miracles and boldly preach the gospel of Jesus Christ. This will
be a time when many people will have yet another opportunity to become
believers.

---

[23] *The Popular Bible Prophecy Commentary*
[24] See Paul Yonggi Cho; *Revelation;* p.107
[25] Jeff Kinley; *As it Was in the Days of Noah;* p.62

"And afterward,
I will pour out my Spirit on all people.
Your sons and daughters will prophesy,
your old men will dream dreams,
your young men will see visions.
Even on my servants, both men and women,
I will pour out my Spirit in those days.
I will show wonders in the heavens
and on the earth,
blood and fire and billows of smoke.
The sun will be turned to darkness
and the moon to blood
before the coming of the great and dreadful day of the
LORD.
And everyone who calls
on the name of the LORD will be saved;
for on Mount Zion and in Jerusalem
there will be deliverance,
as the LORD has said,
even among the survivors
whom the LORD calls. "

Joel 2:28-32

After 1,260 days of prophesying, the beast from the Abyss attacks and kills them (Rev.11:9). He leaves their bodies decomposing in the public square for three and a half days, during which time "some from every people, tribe, language and nation will gaze on their bodies and refuse them burial" (Rev.11:9). Once again we have a prophecy that can be literally fulfilled now by means of satellite television and the Internet. This cruel act delights everybody and they "celebrate by sending each other gifts, because these two prophets had tormented those who live on the earth" (Rev.11:10).

Although the death of the two witnesses appears to have silenced their gospel message, there is a dramatic development. God not only resurrects them from the dead but they ascend to heaven in a cloud, which is witnessed by all their enemies and probably recorded on television for the whole world to see.

But after the three and a half days the breath of life from God
entered them, and they stood on their feet, and terror struck

those who saw them. Then they heard a loud voice from heaven saying to them, "Come up here." And they went up to heaven in a cloud, while their enemies looked on.

Revelation 11:11-12

Once the two prophets ascend to heaven, a severe earthquake takes place and a tenth of the city of Jerusalem collapses.

Seven thousand people were killed in the earthquake, and the survivors were terrified and gave glory to the God of heaven.

Revelation 11:13

The Seventh Trumpet

Once the angel sounds the <u>seventh</u> trumpet, spontaneous worship breaks out in heaven to announce the good news that God and his Son Jesus Christ will reign for evermore.

The seventh angel sounded his trumpet, and there were loud voices in heaven, which said: "The kingdom of the world has become the kingdom of our Lord and of his Messiah, and he will reign for ever and ever."

Revelation 11:15

The moment of anticipating Christ's eternal reign concludes with the opening of the temple of God, and within the temple the ark of the covenant can be seen. This revealing is accompanied by "flashes of lightning, rumblings, peals of thunder, an earthquake and a severe hailstorm" (Rev.11:19). This is the prelude to the final seven bowl judgements which are God's most severe judgements of all.

The Final Warning

God gives those left on earth a final opportunity to repent and respond to the gospel. After sending the 144,000 Jewish evangelists and the two witnesses (preachers) God sends an angel to preach the gospel to everybody throughout the world; *evangelion* in the Greek means the 'good news'.

Then I saw another angel flying in midair, and he had the eternal gospel to proclaim to those who live on the earth – to every nation, tribe, language and people. He said in a loud voice, "Fear God and give him glory, because the hour of his judgment has come. Worship him who made the heavens, the earth, the sea and the springs of water.

Revelation 14:6-7

This angel will have the unique ability to share the gospel in a "loud voice" so that every single person in every ethnic group, in every country on the planet will hear the gospel message in their own language. Nobody will have any excuse to claim they had not heard the good news of salvation and the call to repentance. This final warning will make it clear that God's judgment is about to commence and everyone needs to respond and worship God who is the creator of everything in the world and the universe.

No individual will be able to stand on the day of judgment and claim, "But I never knew about you, Lord."[26]

The seven bowl judgments that follow take place in the second half of the Great Tribulation and are absolutely horrendous.

Life Under Tribulation: The Seven Bowls

I saw in heaven another great and marvellous sign: seven angels with the seven last plagues – last because with them God's wrath is completed.

Revelation 15:1

The seven angels are given seven bowls and told:

"Go, pour out the seven bowls of God's wrath on the earth."

Revelation 16:1

When the <u>first</u> angel pours out his bowl of plagues on the land, "ugly, festering sores broke out on the people who had the mark of the beast and worshiped its image" (Rev.16:2). This awful punishment is only directed at those people who have taken the mark of the beast and sworn allegiance to Satan; all righteous persons do not suffer these "ulcers, cancerous lesions, or suppurated wounds ... that imply painful or agonizing ulcers that resist healing"[27]. The anguish of suffering festering sores all over their bodies with no treatment available to provide relief is hard to imagine.

---

[26] Jeff Kinley; *As it Was in the Days of Noah;* p.63
[27] Tim LaHaye & Ed Hindson; *The Popular Bible Prophecy Commentary*

49

After the <u>second</u> angel pours out his bowl on the sea, all the seas and oceans "turned into blood like that of a dead person, and every living thing in the sea died" (Rev.16:3). It is difficult to conjure up the spectacle and stench of a further two trillion dead fish rotting on the seashore.

When the <u>third</u> angel pours out his bowl, all the rivers and springs turn to blood. No human can survive without fresh drinking water, which causes death by dehydration in 3-6 days. Drinking blood is toxic to humans and causes death in several unpleasant ways.

> *"You are just in these judgments, O Holy One, you who are and who were, for they have shed the blood of your holy people and your prophets and you have given them blood to drink as they deserve."*
>
> *Revelation 16:6*

After the <u>fourth</u> angel "poured out his bowl on the sun ... the sun was allowed to scorch people with fire" (Rev.16:8). This has been described as "a solar flare that bombards the earth with intense radiation"[28].

> *A solar flare is a tremendous explosion on the sun that happens when energy stored in 'twisted' magnetic fields is suddenly released. They are major events that can trigger radio black-outs around the whole world and long lasting radiation storms in the upper atmosphere.*
>
> *European Space Agency[29]*

It is hard to visualise this scene of people suffering ugly, itching sores and being unable to quench their incapacitating thirst. In addition, they are suffering severe sunburn and finding there is no relief available. The reaction of these unbelievers is to curse God, as they realise he has the power to cause or stop the plagues "but they refused to repent and glorify him" (Rev.16:9).

> *The <u>fifth</u> angel poured out his bowl on the throne of the beast, and its kingdom was plunged into darkness. People gnawed their tongues in agony and cursed the God of heaven because*

---

[28] Ibid
[29] *www.esa.int*

of their pains and their sores, but they refused to repent of what they had done.

Revelations 16:10-11 (underlining added)

It must be horrific to experience agonising pain in pitch black darkness without medication to provide relief. However, the real tragedy is that they fail to recognise Jesus is Lord of all; they have such rebellious hearts that all these agonising afflictions have no effect on their willingness to repent.

The <u>sixth</u> angel pours out his bowl "on the great river Euphrates and its waters dried up to prepare the way for the kings of the east" (Rev.16:12). This is in preparation for the battle of Armageddon which will take place in an area 60 miles north of Jerusalem in the southern part of Galilee, known as the Plain of Esdraelon. Satan will respond by sending three demonic spirts to summon an enormous army...

> *...[from] the kings of the whole world, to gather them for the battle on the great day of God Almighty ... Then they gathered the kings together to the place that in Hebrew is called Armageddon.*
>
> *Revelation 16:14,16*

The Seventh Bowl

When the <u>seventh</u> angel pours out his bowl of wrath into the air, a loud voice from the throne of God's temple will thunder, "It is done." (Rev.16:17b) This will culminate in a deafening and frightening earthquake which will be cataclysmic and cause catastrophic tsunamis.

> *Then there came flashes of lightning, rumblings, peals of thunder and a severe earthquake. No earthquake like it has ever occurred since mankind had been on earth, so tremendous was the quake. The great city split into three parts, and the cities of the nations collapsed.*
>
> *Revelation 16:18-19*

Seismologists consider the 'Hayland fault' to be the most dangerous in the world because it runs through ten densely populated cities. Homes, schools, churches, the Oakland Zoo and various stadiums are in the danger zone. In the Middle East there are four major tectonic plates: Nubia (Africa), Sinai (Israel), Arabia and Anotolia (Turkey). Israel is riddled with faults because it sits on the Sinai microplate and its landscape would be changed by these momentous changes; this is exactly what Zechariah prophesied would happen.

> *On that day his feet will stand on the Mount of Olives, east of Jerusalem, and the Mount of Olives will be split in two from east to west, forming a great valley, with half of the valley moving north and half moving south.*
>
> Zechariah 14:4

This event will create a very large valley and the river will divide in Jerusalem and become two great rivers.

> *On that day living water will flow out from Jerusalem, half of it east to the Dead Sea and half of it west to the Mediterranean Sea, in summer and in winter.*
>
> Zechariah 14:8

As prophesied, the Dead Sea will become a great place for fishing as there will be large stocks of fish in there.

> *"This water flows towards the eastern region and goes down into the Arabah, where it enters the Dead Sea. When it empties into the sea, the salty water there becomes fresh. Swarms of living creatures will live wherever the river flows. There will be a large number of fish, because this water flows there and makes the salt-water fresh; so where the water flows everything will live. Fishermen will stand along the shore; from En Gedi to En Eglaim there will be places for spreading nets. The fish will be of many kinds – like the fish of the Mediterranean Sea."*
>
> Ezekiel 47:8-10

The Arabah in Hebrew means 'a desolate and dry area' and is in the Jordan Valley (see Josh.18:18). It is geographically south of the Dead Sea basin which forms part of the border between Israel to the west and Jordan to the east. En Gedi in Hebrew means 'spring of the kid (young goat)' and is an oasis in Hazezon-Tamar (see 2.Chr.20:2).[30] En Eglaim

---

[30] Source: Wikipedia

means the 'fountain of two calves' (see Ez.47:10) and is a place in Palestine.[31]

Worse will follow. This devastating earthquake and pummelling from the sky by hailstones will be felt globally. The mountains will fall apart and existing islands will disappear as the earth experiences these prophesied tremendous topographical changes. The most visible evidence of these changes on the earth will be that the temple in Jerusalem will stand on the highest mountain and will tower above all the hills as prophesied 2,600 years previously (see Is.2:2).

> *Every island fled away and the mountains could not be found.*
> *From the sky huge hailstones, each weighing about a hundred*
> *pounds, fell on people. And they cursed God on account of*
> *the plague of hail, because the plague was so terrible.*
>
> *Revelation 16:20-21*

These enormous hailstones will be quite exceptional and absolutely terrifying. Each one weighs 100 pounds and it has been calculated they would measure 29 inches across and arrive at sea level at a speed of 284 miles per hour. The power of these hailstones will completely annihilate anyone they hit and crush anything they strike. They will crash through buildings, destroy and decimate structures, and crush trees, vegetation and natural habitats.

Job informs us God has already prepared these hailstones which are stored in his storehouses, ready to send plummeting to earth at the appointed time.

> *"Have you entered the storehouses of the snow*
> *or seen the storehouses of the hail,*
> *which I reserve for times of trouble,*
> *for days of war and battle?"*
>
> *Job 38:22-23*

There will be one exception when this is all over.

> *Jerusalem will be raised up high from the Benjamin Gate to*
> *the site of the First Gate, to the Corner Gate, and from the*

---

[31] *Strong's Exhaustive Concordance of the Bible*

Tower of Hananel to the royal winepresses, and will remain in its place.

Zechariah 14:10

The horror of these incredible events is difficult to fully appreciate, but this is what has been prophesied will happen. When God decides to give vent to his righteous wrath on sinners who choose to worship and give their allegiance to Satan, then be afraid. However, there is a great message of hope contained within Isaiah's vision concerning Judah and Jerusalem, because he prophesied Jesus Christ's return to earth with all believers to establish his Millennial Reign.

In the last days
   the mountain of the LORD's temple will be established
      as the highest of the mountains;
   it will be exalted above the hills,
      and all nations will stream to it.
Many peoples will come and say,
   "Come, let us go up to the mountain of the LORD,
      to the temple of the God of Jacob.
He will teach us his ways,
      so that we may walk in his paths."
The law will go out from Zion,
      the word of the LORD from Jerusalem.
He will judge between the nations
      and will settle disputes for many peoples.
They will beat their swords into plowshares
      and their spears into pruning hooks.
Nation will not take up sword against nation,
      nor will they train for war anymore.

Isaiah 2:2-4

Points for Reflection

The time of Great Tribulation will be a final opportunity for unbelievers to accept Jesus Christ as their personal saviour and turn to him in repentance, providing they do not swear allegiance to Satan by taking the mark of the beast, as that decision is irreversible. The cost of becoming a believer during the Great Tribulation will almost certainly require the ultimate sacrifice.

God has no intention of putting born again Christians through this awful tribulation as they have chosen to accept Jesus Christ as their personal saviour and to love, serve and follow him. A born again Christian is adopted into God's family as his son and heir and will be spared God's wrath during the Tribulation because they will have been gloriously raptured to enjoy eternal life with their heavenly Father.

Who shall separate us from the love of Christ? Shall trouble or hardship or persecution or famine or nakedness or danger or sword? As it is written:

"For your sake we face death all day long;
we are considered as sheep to be slaughtered."

No, in all these things we are more than conquerors through him who loved us. For I am convinced that neither death nor life, neither angels nor demons, neither the present nor the future, nor any powers, neither height nor depth, nor anything else in all creation, will be able to separate us from the love of God that is in Christ Jesus our Lord.

Romans 8:35-39

This portrayal of life during the Great Tribulation is one of the strongest arguments to prepare for a Pre-Tribulation Rapture, especially since God has promised believers they will not suffer his wrath. It should act as a timely reminder to the church and all believers that they have a duty to take every opportunity to witness to the lost and bring in a harvest of souls before it is too late.

It is clearly prophesied that in the last days the Holy Spirit will be poured out:

"I will pour out my Spirit in those days."

Joel 2:29b

This is reiterated by Luke in Acts:

"'In the last days, God says, I will pour out my Spirit on all people.'"

Acts 2:17

The prophets Ezekiel and Isaiah prophesied:

"I will pour out my Spirit on the people of Israel."

Ezekiel 39:29

"I will pour out my Spirit on your offspring, and my blessing on your descendants."

Isaiah 44:3b

The position can be summed up by Finis Jennings Dake in the following explanation (see 2.Thess.2:7-8):

> *The church will continue to hinder lawlessness until the Rapture. And then the Antichrist will be revealed. This is conclusive proof that the Rapture takes place before Daniel's 70th week and the tribulation of Revelation 6 : 1 until 19 : 21. According to Daniel 9 : 27, Antichrist will be here for 7 years, for he makes a 7 year covenant with Israel. If he is here for 7 years, (which will be the last 7 years of this age) and if he who hinders lawlessness refers to the church and is taken out of the way before he comes, then the Rapture will take place before the last 7 years of this age and before the Antichrist comes at the beginning of those 7 years.*

Finis Jennings Dake [32]

> *"He will enter into a binding and irrevocable covenant with the many for one week (seven years), but in the middle of the week he will stop the sacrifice and grain offering (for the remaining three and one-half years); and on the wing of abominations will come one who makes desolate, even until the complete destruction, one that is decreed, is poured out on the one who causes the horror."*

Daniel 9:27 (AMP)

It is conceivable that the Antichrist may be heading up his government sometime before Daniel's 70th week, as it is only when he enters into a "binding and irrevocable covenant" with Israel that the Tribulation begins.

Let us conclude with a final message of encouragement from the apostle John which is for all born again Christians.

---

[32] *Dake's Annotated Reference Bible: New Testament;* p.230

"Look, I am coming soon! My reward is with me, and I will give to each person according to what they have done."

Revelation 22:12

He who testifies to these things says, "Yes, I am coming soon." Amen. Come Lord Jesus. The grace of the Lord Jesus be with God's people. Amen.

Revelation 22:20

A Personal Challenge for Sceptics

The Bible is clear about the horrific events every unbeliever will face if the Rapture of all Christians occurs before they die. Unbelievers will face seven years of Great Tribulation under the rule of the Antichrist which should serve as a warning of what lies ahead for everyone who rejects Jesus Christ's offer of salvation.

Before a person dies, they must decide whether their destiny will be heaven or hell. The Bible is unequivocal. When unbelievers die, they will face God's judgement. This is when God identifies those who have scorned the claims of Jesus Christ and rejected his offer of salvation, and decides their eternal destiny. If you have rejected the free gift of salvation and are unwilling to repent, then get ready for the Day of Judgement.

For all have sinned and fall short of the glory of God.

Romans 3:23

The Bible is clear about the consequences of being an unrepentant sinner. You will experience eternal conscious punishment in the lake of fire.

For the wages of sin is death, but the gift of God is eternal life in Christ Jesus our Lord.

Romans 6:23

While you are alive there is still time to admit you are a sinner and to ask God for his forgiveness. If you are genuinely sorry, you can ask the Lord Jesus Christ to come into your life, change you and become your Saviour and Lord.

For God so loved the world that he gave his one and only Son, that whoever believes in him shall not perish but have eternal life. For God did not send his Son into the world to condemn the world, but to save the world through him. Whoever believes in him is not condemned, but whoever does not believe stands condemned already because they have not believed in the name of God's one and only Son.

John 3:16-18

If you are challenged by these scriptures and don't wish to face the intense anger of God, you can take the important step of becoming a Christian. Please turn to the Postscript and pray the simple prayer and invite Jesus Christ into your life.

Questions

Why was John told not to write down and reveal what the seven thunders had said to him after the sixth trumpet sounded?

Was the book of Revelation written to tell us what is going to happen or to prepare us for what is going to happen?

How should we respond to the future events set out in the book of Revelation?

The Bible offers positive incentives for believers to persevere and overcome hardship and persecution. Do believers who fail to be overcomers share the same fate as unbelievers?

Can everyone, however great a sinner, qualify to receive God's gift of eternal life (see Rom.6:23)?

_____

_____

_____

_____

Why does God include a stern warning not to "add anything" or "take words away" (Rev.22:18) from this prophecy?

_____

_____

_____

_____

CHAPTER FOUR

Triumphant Heavenly Songs[33]

Introduction

All those who have become born again Christians before the Rapture can have the assurance that they will be spared the wrath of God that unbelievers will experience during the seven years of Tribulation. Instead, they will appear before the judgement seat of Christ "so that each of us may receive what is due for the things done while in the body, whether good or bad" (2.Cor.5:10).

This will be a time of great rejoicing in heaven as believers renew fellowship with other Christians and are reunited with relatives and loved ones that have gone before them.

The joy of meeting our Lord and Saviour Jesus Christ will be compounded by receiving rewards for faithful service and the good deeds undertaken whilst on earth as Christians. This wonderful, blissful time of rejoicing will last for evermore. It will also be a time to prepare for the Second Coming of Jesus Christ, when we will return with him to take on our new responsibilities and roles he has prepared for us during his Millennial Reign of perfect rule.

The apostle John's vision in Revelation includes ten joyful triumphant heavenly songs dedicated to Jesus Christ and our heavenly Father. Praise and worship in heaven will be an unbelievable experience when we can truly exalt his name in thankfulness for his free gift of our salvation and enjoy the overwhelming experience of being sons and heirs with Jesus Christ and living and serving him for evermore.

---

[33] This chapter is an extended version of an article that appeared in *Prophetic Witness,* October 2020

Now if we are children, then we are heirs – heirs of God and co-heirs with Christ, if indeed we share in his sufferings in order that we may also share in his glory.

Romans 8:17

Singing plays a far more prominent role in the book of Revelation than in any other book in the New Testament. As the prophecy of Jesus Christ unfolds, these songs celebrate God's greatness as the Creator and Jesus Christ's redemptive work on the cross. This is accompanied by new heavenly songs of rejoicing that focus on the themes of worship, worthiness and thankfulness. The apostle John describes how he is admitted to the throne room and witnesses spectacular scenes of praise and worship. The Greek word *kainos* means 'fresh' or 'a new kind'[34].

And they sang a new song, saying:
  "You are worthy to take the scroll
    and to open its seals,
  because you were slain,
    and with your blood you purchased for God
    persons from every tribe and language and nation.
  You have made them to be a kingdom and priests to serve our God
    and they will reign on the earth."

Revelation 5:9-10

The First Song

The first song celebrates God's holiness, omnipotence and eternalness. It is sung constantly by the four living creatures who encourage worship and adoration whilst proclaiming the holiness of God. The opening line of this song, "Holy, holy, holy is the Lord God Almighty," is taken from Isaiah 6:3.

"Holy, holy, holy,
the Lord God the Almighty,
who was and is and is to come."

Revelation 4:8 (NRSV)

---

[34] See *The KJV New Testament Greek Lexicon*

At this point the twenty-four elders lay down their crowns before the throne and sing:

> *"You are worthy, our Lord and God,*
> *to receive glory and honor and power,*
> *for you created all things,*
> *and by your will they existed and were created."*

Revelation 4:11 (NRSV)

The Second Song

The second song of worship is directed to Jesus Christ and celebrates his worthiness to open the seven seals. No one is found worthy to open the seals in the whole of heaven or anywhere on the earth. This distresses the apostle John until one of the elders points out the only person who is worthy: Jesus Christ (see Rev.5:3).

> *"See, the Lion of the tribe of Judah, the Root of David, has triumphed. He is able to open the scroll and its seven seals."*

Revelation 5:5

Jesus Christ then becomes the primary focus of worship by the four living creatures and the twenty-four elders, who bow down before him. Holding a harp and a bowl of incense containing the prayers of believers, they rejoice by singing this new song:

> *"You are worthy to take the scroll and to open its seals,*
> *for you were slaughtered and by your blood*
> *you ransomed for God*
> *saints from every tribe and language and people and nation;*
> *you have made them to be a kingdom and priests*
> *serving our God,*
> *and they will reign on earth."*

Revelation 5:9-10 (NRSV)

The Third Song

The third song is another worship song which exalts Jesus Christ, but this time there is a huge increase in the size of the heavenly choir.

> *Ten thousand was the largest single number used in Greek, so thousands upon thousands, and ten thousand times ten*

thousand (NIV) or myriads of myriads (NRSV) is the author's
way of calling them innumerable.

Craig S. Keener[35]

This vast number of angels surrounding the throne join with the four living creatures and twenty-four elders "singing with full voice" (Rev.5:12, NRSV).

> *"Worthy is the Lamb, that was slaughtered*
> *to receive power and wealth and wisdom*
> *and might and honor and glory and blessing!"*

Revelation 5:12 (NRSV)

The Fourth Song

The fourth song is addressed to both God on the throne and Jesus Christ, the Lamb. Jesus Christ who redeemed mankind is placed on an equal footing with God as worthy of all praise. Every living creature in heaven and earth joins in, and the volume of praise and worship is awe-inspiring and indescribable. It has spilled out of heaven to the earth and includes the sea and everything under the sea; even the fish in the sea are offering praise to God and Jesus Christ!

> *"To the one seated on the throne and to the Lamb*
> *be blessing and honor and glory and might,*
> *forever and ever!"*

Revelation 5:13 (NRSV)

The four living creatures join in with:

> *"Amen!"*

Revelation 5:14a (NRSV)

The Fifth Song

The next song of worship is sung after the sixth seal is opened and is again directed to God on the throne and Jesus Christ, the Lamb, by a multitude comprising so many Christians that they cannot be counted. They come from every nation on earth, wearing white robes and holding

---

[35] *The Bible Background Commentary*

palm branches in their hands. They are celebrating the believers who have come out of the Great Tribulation, unblemished and righteous.

> *These are they who have come out of the great tribulation; they have washed their robes and made them white in the blood of the Lamb.*
>
> Revelation 7:14

They celebrate by "holding palm branches", (Rev.7:9) a reminder of the triumphant entry of Jesus into Jerusalem at Passover.

> *They took palm branches and went out to meet him, shouting, "Hosanna! Blessed is he who comes in the name of the Lord!"*
>
> John 12:13

On the first day of the Feast of Tabernacles (Lev.23:34) the Israelites would celebrate their deliverance from captivity in Egypt, with "branches of palm trees" (Lev.23:40, NRSV) "so your descendants will know that I had the Israelites live in temporary shelters when I brought them out of Egypt" (Lev.23:43).[36]

The Sixth Song

The refrain "Salvation comes from the Lord" (Jnh.2:9) was Jonah's prayer inside the huge fish, but this time the multitudes are celebrating and loudly proclaim:

> *"Salvation belongs to our God who is seated on the throne, and to the Lamb!"*
>
> Revelation 7:10 (NRSV)

The heavenly angels, the four elders and twenty-four living creatures, respond by singing:

> *"Amen! Blessing and glory and wisdom and thanksgiving and honor and power and might be to our God for ever and ever. Amen!"*
>
> Revelation 7:12 (NRSV)

---

[36] This feast of celebration is also known as the Feast of Booths (AMP, NRSV) or the Festival of Shelters (NLT) or The Feast of Tabernacles (NIV).

The Seventh Song

When the seventh angel blows his trumpet, loud voices in heaven celebrate.

> *"The kingdom of the world has become the kingdom of our Lord and of his Messiah, and he will reign forever and ever."*
>
> *Revelation 11:15 (NRSV)*

The twenty-four elders respond by worshipping God, who reigns supreme and will dispense perfect justice, with this seventh song.

> *"We give you thanks, Lord God Almighty,*
> *who are and who were,*
> *for you have taken your great power*
> *and begun to reign.*
> *The nations raged,*
> *but your wrath has come,*
> *and the time for judging the dead,*
> *for rewarding your servants, the prophets*
> *and saints and all who fear your name,*
> *both small and great,*
> *and for destroying those who destroy the earth."*
>
> *Revelation 11:17-18 (NRSV)*

The Eighth New Mysterious Song (Rev.14:3-5)

The mysterious, undisclosed new song is directed towards the throne of God and the four living creatures and the elders. This unique song is sung by the 144,000 believers in heaven who have God's name written on their foreheads. One of God's mysteries is that although John heard this new song, the words of the song are not disclosed and are reserved solely for this special group of righteous believers to learn.

> *No one could learn that song except the one hundred forty-four thousand who have been redeemed from the earth. It is these who have not defiled themselves with women, for they are virgins; these follow the Lamb wherever he goes. They have been redeemed from humankind as first fruits for God and the Lamb, and in their mouth no lie was found; for they are blameless.*
>
> *Revelation 14:3-5 (NRSV)*

The motivation for people offering the "first fruits" to God was one of thankfulness at harvest-time as God had met all their needs.

> *"When you enter the land to which I am taking you, and you eat the food of the land, present a portion as an offering to the LORD."*
>
> *Numbers 15:18-19*

The prophet Jeremiah recalls a time when the Israelites worshipped God and honoured his commandments.

> *"I remember the devotion of your youth,*
> *your love as a bride,*
> *how you followed me in the wilderness,*
> *in a land not sown.*
> *Israel was holy to the LORD,*
> *the first fruits of his harvest."*
>
> *Jeremiah 2:2-3 (NRSV)*

The "first fruits" were a sample of the entire harvest and the sacrifices to the Lord were to be the best and unblemished "first fruits" of their produce, fruit, oxen and sheep.

> *But Christ has indeed been raised from the dead, the first fruits of those who have fallen asleep. For since death came through a man, the resurrection of the dead comes also through a man. For as in Adam all die, so in Christ all will be made alive. But each in turn: Christ, the first fruits; then, when he comes, those who belong to him.*
>
> *1 Corinthians 15:20-23*

The Ninth Song

The ninth song is addressed to both God and Jesus Christ and is sung prior to the final outpouring of God's wrath on all those who had taken the mark of the beast. This song celebrates what the apostle John describes as "another great and marvellous sign: seven angels with the seven last plagues – last, because with them God's wrath is completed" (Rev.15:1).

Those who had been victorious over the beast "held harps given them by God and sang the song of God's servant Moses and of the Lamb" (Rev.15:2-3). The Song of Moses was one of triumph – victory over

Pharaoh and his armies (see Ex.15:1-18). The Song of the Lamb is also one of triumph – victory over Satan and all the enemies of God and man.

> *"Great and amazing are your deeds,*
>   *Lord God the Almighty!*
> *Just and true are your ways,*
>   *King of the nations!*
> *Lord, who will not fear*
>   *and glorify your name?*
> *For you alone are holy.*
> *All nations will come*
>   *and worship before you,*
> *for your judgments have been revealed."*

Revelation 15:3-4 (NRSV)

The Tenth Song

This comes after the rejoicing of the final destruction of Babylon. The twenty-four elders and the four living creatures fall down and worship God.

> *And from the throne came a voice saying,*
>   *"Praise our God,*
>   *all you his servants,*
>   *and all who fear him,*
>   *small and great."*

Revelation 19:5 (NRSV)

> *Then I heard what sounded like a great multitude, like the roar*
> *of rushing waters and like loud peals of thunder, shouting:*
>   *"Hallelujah!*
>   *For our Lord God Almighty reigns.*
>   *Let us rejoice and be glad*
>   *and give him the glory!*
>   *For the wedding of the Lamb has come,*
>   *and his bride has made herself ready.*
>   *Fine linen, bright and clean,*
>   *was given her to wear."*
> *(Fine linen stands for the righteous acts of God's holy people.)*

Revelation 19:6-8

Then John is told that those invited to the wedding supper of the Lamb are blessed and that, "These are the true words of God." (Rev.19:9b)

Conclusion

These joyful 'new songs' honour Jesus Christ as a full member of the godhead and celebrate his worthiness to receive praise and worship. They provide the believer with a glimpse of how wonderful, uplifting and glorious worship in heaven will be. This will be a time of great rejoicing as we live with Jesus Christ for ever and ever.

> *The one who testifies to these things says, "Surely I am coming soon."*
> *Amen. Come, Lord Jesus!*
>
> *Revelation 22:20 (NRSV)*

In the next chapter we explore the significance of the most apocalyptic event in the history of the earth, which is at the Second Coming of Jesus Christ. We examine the promises of Jesus concerning this event, how it was prophesied in detail by Isaiah 2,750 years ago and how it ushers in awful judgement for unbelievers who have rejected the love of Jesus Christ. The events that unfold are truly awful, but the good news is that Satan is banished to the Abyss for a thousand years. These events are in sharp contrast to the promises that will be fulfilled for believers, who are longing for the return of Jesus Christ.

Questions

Do the songs and hymns we sing in church celebrate God's character, his mighty power and faithfulness?

_____

_____

_____

Do our praise and worship songs help us to be thankful for God's gracious and powerful rule?

_____

_____

_____

Do our worship songs help us take a firm stand against Satan and enable us to be faithful witnesses to God's saving power, as contained in the truth of the gospel?

_____

_____

_____

Do our worship songs encourage us to hold fast to God's commandments and Jesus' teaching?

_____

_____

_____

Do the songs we sing inspire and encourage us to be victorious in our daily lives?

_____

_____

_____

Does our praise and worship give us a glimpse of heaven and help us focus on our eternal heavenly home?

_____

_____

_____

CHAPTER FIVE

The Second Coming of Jesus Christ

Introduction

It may surprise you to learn that prophecy makes up 28% of the Bible.[37] The Old Testament Bible contains 127 prophecies about the coming Messiah, comprising 574 verses, which have been fulfilled down to every last detail,[38] but there over 325 prophecies about the Second Coming of Jesus Christ. There is no reason to doubt they will all be fulfilled and it will happen exactly as it has been recorded in the Bible.

When Jesus Commissioned the Lord's Supper, he said to remember his death until he returns again:

> *For whenever you eat this bread and drink this cup, you proclaim the Lord's death until he comes.*
>
> *1 Corinthians 11:26*

As we take communion, we remember with gratitude his death on the cross when Jesus paid the price for our sins. Do we also remember his promise to return? We should feel encouraged that the day of his Second Coming is drawing closer when he will finally deal with Satan who will be "thrown into the lake of burning sulfur" (Rev.20:10).

Jesus Prophesies His Second Coming

Several times Jesus promised that he would come again for believers. These include the Mount of Olives Discourse, his appearance before the Sanhedrin prior to his crucifixion and when he ascended to heaven.

---

[37] Tim LaHaye & Thomas Ice; *Charting the End Times*
[38] John Barton Payne; *Encyclopaedia of Biblical Prophecy*

THE OLIVET DISCOURSE

At the Olivet Discourse (Matt.24-25) Jesus answered his disciples' questions concerning, "...when will this happen, and what will be the signs of your coming and of the end of the age?" (Matt.24:3) Jesus explained in detail all the signs that will herald his Second Coming.

He prophesied the temple would be destroyed (fulfilled in A.D. 70) and that there be world wars, rumours of wars, famines, pestilence, earthquakes, false Messiahs, false prophets, the Jews would be hated and persecuted by every country, many believers would become apostate, false prophets and Messiahs would appear, there would be an increase in wickedness, and the gospel message would be preached throughout the world before his Glorious Appearing (see Matt.24:4-14). The return of Jesus Christ will be to destroy all the enemies of the Jews, to judge the nations, unbelievers and Satan and the two beasts, all of whom he will punish. There will be no mistaking his appearing because he will announce his arrival in spectacular fashion and everyone will witness this world-changing event.

> *"Immediately after the distress of those days 'the sun will be darkened, and the moon will not give its light; the stars will fall from the sky, and the heavenly bodies will be shaken.' Then will appear the sign of the Son of Man in heaven. And then all the peoples of the north will mourn when they see the Son of Man coming on the clouds of heaven, with power and great glory."*
>
> *Matthew 24:29-30*

One of Christ's first actions will be to gather together all those who became believers during the Great Tribulation and avoided being murdered by the Antichrist and beast.

> *"He will send his angels with a loud trumpet call, and they will gather his elect from the four winds, from one end of the heavens to the other."*
>
> *Matthew 24:31*

JESUS APPEARS AT THE SANHEDRIN

After Judas Iscariot betrayed Jesus to the chief priests for £2,000 (thirty denarius), Judas arrived at the Garden of Gethsemane with a large

73

mob armed with swords and clubs to arrest Jesus. They took him to Caiaphas the high priest, where the whole Sanhedrin had assembled.

> *The chief priests and the whole Sanhedrin were looking for false evidence against Jesus so that they could put him to death. But they did not find any, though many false witnesses came forward.*
>
> *Matthew 26:59-60a*

> *Many testified falsely against him, but their statements did not agree.*
>
> *Mark 14:56*

> *Finally two came forward and declared, "This fellow said, 'I am able to destroy the temple of God and rebuild it in three days.'"*

> *Then the high priest stood up and said to Jesus, "Are you not going to answer? What is this testimony that these men are bringing against you?" But Jesus remained silent. The high priest said to him, "I charge you under oath by the living God: Tell us if you are the Messiah, the Son of God."*
>
> *Matthew 26:60b-63*

Although Jesus would not demean himself by answering their false accusations, he did provide a direct answer to whether he was the Messiah. Jesus Christ replied by quoting from Daniel's prophecy (see Dan.7:13-14).

> *"You have said so," Jesus replied. "But I say to all of you: From now on you will see the Son of Man sitting at the right hand of the Mighty One and coming on the clouds of heaven."*

> *Then the high priest tore his clothes and said, "He has spoken blasphemy! Why do we need any more witnesses? Look, now you have heard the blasphemy. What do you think?" "He is worthy of death," they answered.*
>
> *Matthew 26:64-66*

His response enraged the Sanhedrin so much that they disregarded proper judicial process and abused their powers, convicting Jesus of blasphemy. They recommended to Pilate the Roman Governor that he be sentenced to death. When Jesus appeared before Pilate they accused him of claiming to be the King of the Jews, a charge that was treasonous and a direct challenge to the Roman authorities.

JESUS AT HIS ASCENSION

Immediately prior to his ascension to heaven, Jesus told his disciples they would receive power when the Holy Spirit comes on them, to be his witnesses to the whole world.

> *"But you will receive power when the Holy Spirit comes on you; and you will be my witnesses in Jerusalem, and in all Judea and Samaria, and to the ends of the earth."*
>
> *After he said this, he was taken up before their very eyes and a cloud hid him from their sight.*
>
> *They were looking intently up into the sky as he was going, when suddenly two men dressed in white stood beside them. "Men of Galilee," they said, "why do you stand here looking into the sky? This same Jesus, who has been taken from you into heaven, will come back in the same way you have seen him go into heaven."*
>
> *Acts 1:8-11*

The disciples witnessed his literal, physical bodily ascension to heaven. At the Second Coming of Jesus Christ he will return the same way and descend through the clouds with his huge heavenly army – an event that will be witnessed by the whole world.

Waiting for the Glorious Appearing

The return of Jesus Christ did not happen as soon as many had hoped. They were hoping he would return during their lifetimes. Peter reminded them Jesus always keeps his promises and his Second Coming will be like a thief coming to rob your house; he will come when you least expect it.

> *The Lord is not slow in keeping his promise, as some understand slowness. Instead he is patient with you, not wanting anyone to perish, but everyone to come to repentance.*
>
> *2 Peter 3:9*

Time is of no consequence to God, as he counts time differently to humans who need calendars and clocks to regulate their lives.

*With the Lord a day is like a thousand years, and a thousand
years are like a day.*

2 Peter 3:8

God wants everybody in our sinful world to repent and be saved;
although he knows many will choose not to respond to his invitation to
repent and be born again.

*But the day of the Lord will come like a thief. The heavens will
disappear with a roar; the elements will be destroyed by fire,
and the earth and everything done in it will be laid bare.*

2 Peter 3:10

The day of the Lord follows the Tribulation and will be a truly
awesome event that will spell the end of the world as we know it.

*Since everything will be destroyed in this way, what kind of
people ought you to be? You ought to live holy and godly lives
as you look forward to the day of God and speed its coming.
That day will bring about the destruction of the heavens by
fire, and the elements will melt in the heat.*

2 Peter 3:11-12

In the meantime, Peter urges us to live holy lives and look forward in
hope and eager anticipation to Jesus' return. He wants us to take on
board his encouraging prophetic words about our glorious future, which
are given to motivate us, and to envisage the joy of living in a perfect
heaven and earth as members of God's family.

*But in keeping with his promise we are looking forward to a
new heaven and a new earth, where righteousness dwells.*

2 Peter 3:13

Peter is looking beyond the Millennial Reign of Jesus Christ to the
day when he establishes a completely "new heaven and a new earth"
(Rev.21:1). There will be a new holy city of Jerusalem that will descend
from heaven.

*"God's dwelling place is now among the people, and he will
dwell with them. They will be his people, and God himself will
be with them and be their God."*

Revelation 21:3

This is the time when sin, suffering, pain and death will no longer trouble believers, as we live with our heavenly Father and Jesus Christ for evermore.

Isaiah's Prophecies of the Second Coming of Jesus Christ

The account in Revelation of John's vision provides an outline of these final days which were prophesied by Isaiah 2,750 years earlier in the years 740-701 B.C. Isaiah was standing on a mountain in Israel looking eastward towards the land of Edom when he saw a magnificent but blood-stained figure approaching him in glory and splendour. Isaiah did not have the understanding of prophetic knowledge of the last days we have today, to recognise that this person with his "garments stained crimson" was the Lord Jesus Christ, the coming Messiah – so Isaiah initiated a conversation with a series of questions:

> *Who is this coming from Edom,*
> *from Bozrah, with his garments stained crimson?*
> *Who is this, robed in splendor,*
> *striding forward in the greatness of his strength?*
> *"It is I, proclaiming victory,*
> *mighty to save."*
> *Why are your garments red,*
> *like those of one treading the winepress?*
>
> *Isaiah 63:1-3*

It becomes clear that during the battle Jesus Christ fought in the land of Edom at the city of Bozrah, the blood stains were caused when the life-blood of his enemies splattered his clothes staining his clothing when he trampled upon them.

> *"I have trodden the winepress alone;*
> *from the nations no one was with me.*
> *I trampled them in my anger*
> *and trod them down in my wrath;*
> *their blood splattered my garments,*
> *and I stained all my clothing.*
> *It was for me the day of vengeance;*
> *the year for me to redeem had come.*
> *I looked, but there was no one to help,*
> *I was appalled that no one gave support;*

so my own arm achieved salvation for me,
and my own wrath sustained me.
I trampled the nations in my anger;
in my wrath I made them drunk
and poured their blood on the ground."

Isaiah 63:4-6

On Jesus Christ's return his first priority is to save the faithful one-third remnant of the Jews for whom he had made provision by taking them to a place of safety. These survivors of the Great Tribulation fled to the land of Edom to take refuge in the city of Bozrah, and this is where Jesus Christ singlehandedly defeats the mighty armies that assembled to destroy the Jewish remnant.

The current population of Israel is 8,655,500[39] and means up to 5.77 million Jews may be killed by the Antichrist, which equates to the genocide that occurred during the holocaust at the hands of the Nazis. This horrific scenario prophesied by Zechariah, and confirmed in John's vision, means that using these figures as a guide, the faithful remnant may be up to 2.8 million Jews.

"Strike the shepherd,
and the sheep will be scattered,
and I will turn my hand against the little ones.
In the whole land," declares the LORD,
"two-thirds will be struck down and perish;
yet one-third will be left in it.
This third I will put into the fire; I
will refine them like silver
and test them like gold.
They will call on my name
and I will answer them;
I will say, 'They are my people,'
and they will say, 'The LORD is our God.'"

Zechariah 13:7b-9

Amir Tsarfati maintains the "Tribulation is for Israel's salvation"[40]. In the first half of the Tribulation, Israel is completely deceived by the

---

[39] Source: The United Nations
[40] Amir Tsarfati; *The Day Approaching*

Antichrist who confirms a covenant between Israel and the rest of the world. The Jews realise they have been deceived when he desecrates the holy temple and demands to be worshipped as God. Once they realise their mistake, they refuse to worship him, and the Antichrist responds by taking steps to exterminate them all.

> *She gave birth to a son, a male child who "will rule all the nations with an iron scepter." And her child was snatched up to God and to his throne. The woman fled into the wilderness to a place prepared for her by God, where she might be taken care of for 1,260 days.*
>
> *Revelation 12:5-6*

The imagery used needs some explanation. The woman who gives birth represents Israel and the male child is Jesus Christ and is identified as the one who ascends to heaven following his earthly ministry. He is now seated at the right hand of God until the time for his return comes, when he will come in all his majesty and power to eliminate his enemies. Afterwards he "will rule the nations with an iron scepter" from Jerusalem throughout the Millennium. The remnant of Israel will be protected by God as they flee to the wilderness for the duration of the second half of the Great Tribulation (1,260 days).

> *But the two wings of the great eagle were given to the woman, so that she could fly into the wilderness to her place, where she was nourished for a time and times and half a time (three and one-half years), away from the presence of the serpent (Satan).*
>
> *Revelation 12:14 (AMP)*

God also prevents a catastrophe overtaking the fleeing Jews:

> *[Satan] spewed water like a river, to overtake the woman and sweep her away with the torrent. But the earth helped the woman by opening its mouth and swallowing the river that the dragon had spewed out of his mouth.*
>
> *Revelation 12:15-16*

The remnant of the Jews are able to escape because God protects them and keeps them safely out of the dragon's (that is, Satan's) reach.

It is a great mistake for countries to come against the nation of Israel, because Israel is the apple of God's eye, his special, chosen people.

"...whoever touches you touches the apple of his eye – I will raise my hand against them."

Zechariah 2:8

In *The Miracle that is Israel* by Phil Davies, he demonstrates how God has protected the fledging nation of Israel when it was born on 14 May 1948, which fulfilled Isaiah's prophecy, "Shall a land be born in one day?" (Is.66:8, NRSV) Within 12 hours of its birth the country was under attack from Egypt, Lebanon, Syria, Jordan and Iraq. God delivered Israel against overwhelming odds and he has repeated his protection during the Suez crisis, the Six Day War, the Yon Kippur War and against its many adversaries ever since.

God does not forget the sins of those who come and try to destroy his nation and harm his chosen people. Malachi prophesies that Edom will be called "the Wicked Land, a people always under the wrath of the LORD" (Mal.1:4). There will be an everlasting punishment against Edom to remind everybody not to try to destroy the nation of Israel, as it is protected by Almighty God. He is always willing to fight on her behalf and seek vengeance against those who persecute his chosen people.

For the LORD has a day of vengeance,
a year of retribution, to uphold Zion's cause.
Edom's streams will be turned into pitch,
her dust into burning sulfur;
her land will become blazing pitch!
It will not be quenched night or day;
its smoke will rise forever.
From generation to generation it will lie desolate;
no one will ever pass through it again.

Isaiah 34:8-10

The land of Edom, which is now southern Jordan, will remain a desolate land because of its sins against Israel, and God will never allow the land to recover. It will no longer be a land where humans or animals can live; even animals cannot live in a place of "blazing pitch" and "burning sulfur".

The creatures of the desert will encounter jackals
And the hairy goat will call to its kind;
Indeed, Lilith (night demon) will settle there

And find herself a place of rest.

Isaiah 34:14 (AMP)

The Popular Bible Prophecy Commentary explains the meaning of the future desolation of Edom which will be a place inhabited by demons.

> *The word translated 'hairy goat' means 'demons in goat form,' and the word translated 'night monster' means 'night demons.' Like Babylon, Edom will also be an abode of demons.*

Once the forces of the Antichrist that come to the city of Bozrah to destroy the Jewish remnant have been destroyed, Jesus Christ turns his attention to rescuing those remaining in the city of Jerusalem.

> *"The LORD will save the dwellings of Judah first, so that the honor of the house of David and of Jerusalem's inhabitants may not be greater than that of Judah. On that day the LORD will shield those who live in Jerusalem, so that the feeblest among them will be like David, and the house of David, will be like God, like the angel of the LORD going before them. On that day I will destroy all the nations that attack Jerusalem."*

Zechariah 12:7-9

The prophesies are quite specific as to the how, when, why and where Jesus Christ will deal with those who persecute his holy people.

> *"I will gather all nations*
> *and bring them down to the Valley of Jehoshaphat.*
> *There I will put them on trial*
> *for what they did to my inheritance, my people Israel*
> *because they scattered my people among the nations*
> *and divided up my land."*

Joel 3:2-3

Judgement will surely follow for the nations that have persecuted the nation of Israel.

> *"Let the nations be roused;*
> *let them advance into the Valley of Jehoshaphat,*
> *for there I will sit*
> *to judge all the nations on every side."*

Joel 3:12

After the crushing defeat of his enemies, Jesus Christ descends to the Mount of Olives. The victory descent results in a tremendous earthquake that splits the mountain in two and creates a valley for the Jews to escape Jerusalem before it collapses.

> *On that day his feet will stand on the Mount of Olives, east of Jerusalem, and the Mount of Olives will be split in two from east to west, forming a great valley, with half of the mountain moving north and half moving south. You will flee by my mountain valley, for it will extend to Azel.*
>
> Zechariah 14:4-5a

> *When the Messiah comes to Jerusalem it is only after He has fought against the nations, and His coming upon the Mount of Olives is not the initial point of His return, but the final aspect to it. When He returns to Bozrah he will initiate the conflict with the armies that have come against the Jewish people, and once the fighting ends in the Valley of Jehoshaphat, he will then descend onto the Mount of Olives.*
>
> Tim LaHaye & Ed Hindson[41]

The catastrophic earthquake that takes place will rearrange the geography of the area completely and all the land from Geba to Rimmon south of Jerusalem will be changed from the mountainous area it is today into a flat plain like the Arabah.

> *On that day living water will flow out from Jerusalem, half of it east to the Dead Sea and half of it west to the Mediterranean Sea, in summer and in winter. The LORD will be king over the whole earth. On that day there will be one LORD, and his name the only name. The whole land, from Geba to Rimmon, south of Jerusalem, will become like the Arabah. But Jerusalem will be raised up high from the Benjamin Gate to the site of the First Gate, to the Corner Gate, and from the Tower of Hananel to the royal winepresses, and will remain in its place. It will be inhabited; never again will it be destroyed. Jerusalem will be secure.*
>
> Zechariah 14:8-11

---

[41] *The Popular Bible Prophecy Commentary*

These enormous topographical changes mean that in the Millennium, the city of Jerusalem will be situated upon the highest mountain in the world.

> *Now it will come to pass that*
> *In the last days*
> *The mountain of the house of the Lord*
> *Will be (firmly) established as the highest of the mountains,*
> *And will be exalted above the hills;*
> *And all the nations will stream to it.*
> *And many peoples shall come and say,*
> *"Come, let us go up to the mountain of the Lord,*
> *To the house (temple) of the God of Jacob;*
> *That he may teach us His ways*
> *And that we may walk in His paths."*
> *For the law will go out from Zion*
> *And the word of the LORD from Jerusalem.*
>
> *Isaiah 2:2-3 (AMP)*

Zechariah provides further details as to how Israel's enemies will be destroyed at Armageddon.

> *Their flesh will rot while they are still standing on their feet, their eyes will rot in their sockets, and their tongues will rot in their mouths.*
>
> *Zechariah 14:12*

All their livestock will be affected by the same plague, making them completely useless and completely inedible. During the great panic and confusion that envelopes the armies of the Antichrist, they attack and destroy each other.

The emboldened and energised Jewish forces take advantage of this chaos to completely destroy the enemy and, according to Tim La Haye and Ed Hindson, "The Jewish people will collect the spoils rather than become the spoils of the enemy."[42]

---

[42] See Tim LaHaye & Ed Hindson; *The Popular Bible Prophecy Commentary;* p.314

> *Judah too will fight at Jerusalem. The wealth of all the surrounding nations will be collected – great quantities of gold and silver and clothing.*
>
> *Zechariah 14:14*

The Glorious Appearing

Jesus Christ's Glorious Appearing will not be a time of joy for the unsaved but a time of great sorrow because the day of God's wrath and vengeance has come. At the end of the Great Tribulation, "they will see the Son of Man coming in a cloud with power and great glory" (Lk.21:27). This Glorious Appearing of Jesus Christ takes place following many momentous signs and wonders appearing in the heavens, in the sea and on the earth.

> *"There will be signs in the sun, moon and stars. On the earth, nations will be in anguish and perplexity at the roaring and tossing of the sea."*
>
> *Luke 24:25*

> *"Immediately after the distress of those days the sun will be darkened, and the moon will not give its light; the stars will fall from the sky, and heavenly bodies will be shaken."*
>
> *Matthew 24:29*

Everyone on the earth will witness these unexpected events:

> *"For as lightning that comes from the east is visible even in the west, so will be the coming of the Son of Man."*
>
> *Matthew 24:27*

Unbelievers will be frightened because they will be expecting judgement after all the pain and anguish they have experienced, particularly after the seven bowls are poured out.

> *"Then will appear the sign of the Son of Man in heaven. And then all the peoples of the earth will mourn when they see the Son of Man coming on the clouds of heaven, with power and great glory."*
>
> *Matthew 24:30*

The appearance of the Lord will be a spectacular and awesome event. It will be unexpected and a shock to most of the world and a wake-up call for those in Israel who rejected the Messiah when he first came 2,000 years ago. Those who became believers, "the elect", during the Great Tribulation and avoided attempts by the Antichrist to kill them, will be gathered together as part of God's family.

"And he will send his angels and gather his elect from the four winds, from the ends of the earth to the ends of the heavens."

Mark 13:27

In John's vision he provides a graphic description of Jesus Christ's triumphant return to earth riding on a white horse. Jesus Christ is called "Faithful and True" and he appears fully prepared for battle with a sharp sword in his mouth and dressed in a robe dipped in blood. His eyes blaze like fire and he wears many crowns upon his head. Following behind are the armies of God riding white horses and dressed in fine linen robes. They are the church triumphant, who have returned to earth to enjoy his divine and perfect rule.

I saw heaven standing open and there before me was a white horse, whose rider is called Faithful and True. With justice he judges and wages war. His eyes are like blazing fire, and on his head are many crowns. He has a name written on him that no one knows but he himself. He is dressed in a robe dipped in blood, and his name is the Word of God.

Revelation 19:11-13

Jesus Christ will come in great authority wearing "many crowns" which represent his great authority. His eyes like "blazing fire" represent his absolute righteousness and determination to discern the Truth about his deceitful, ungodly enemies whom he will judge accordingly. He will arrive in his full majesty and power and declare his true nature and awesome power. He is the "KING OF KINGS AND LORD OF LORDS" (Rev.19:16b).

His name "the Word of God" comes from the Greek word *logos* meaning 'the expression' and represents the infallible, authoritative, absolute truth of the Bible. It is an expression of the full deity of Jesus Christ.

In the beginning was the Word, and the Word was with God, and the Word was God. He was with God in the Beginning.

John 1:1-2

He also has a name that "no one knows but he himself", but we know it will be a name above every other name, a name that reveals his true glory, majesty and unfathomable greatness.

No one has ever seen God, but the one and only Son, who is himself God and is in closest relationship with the Father, has made him known.

John 1:18

The armies of heaven were following him, riding on white horses and dressed in fine linen, white and clean.

Revelation 19:14

"The armies of heaven" are the saints in glory, which is the church, the bride of Christ.

These armies may also include holy angels who come to carry out the Lord's authority on earth as mentioned in Matthew 25:31.

Tim LaHaye & Ed Hindson[43]

They are not clothed in battledress because they will not be required to fight. The Lord Jesus Christ will defeat his enemies with his voice, which is his sharp sword.

See the Lord is coming with thousands upon thousands of his holy ones to judge everyone, and to convict all of them of all the ungodly acts they have committed in their ungodliness, and of all the defiant words ungodly sinners have spoken against him.

Jude :14-15

The Battle of Armageddon

The final battle of Armageddon takes place where the armies of the Antichrist, False Prophet and Satan are completely defeated.

Then I saw the beast and the kings of the earth and their armies gathered together to wage war against the rider on the horse and his army.

Revelation 19:19

---

[43] *The Popular Bible Prophecy Commentary;* p.537

There is absolutely no doubt about the outcome of this battle! Jesus Christ knows He will be victorious, and an angel issues an invitation to all the birds to attend a fantastic feast where they can gorge themselves on the flesh of His enemies.

> *And I saw an angel standing in the sun, who cried in a loud voice to all the birds flying in mid-air, "Come, gather together for the great supper of God, so that you may eat the flesh of kings, generals, and the mighty, of horses and their riders, and the flesh of all people, free and slave, great and small."*
>
> *Revelation 19:17-18*

Once the Battle of Armageddon commences, it is short-lived, but the consequences are devastating. Everybody in Satan's army is slaughtered; no one is left alive apart from the Antichrist, the False Prophet and Satan.

> *The beast was captured, and with it the false prophet who had performed the signs on its behalf ... The two of them were thrown alive into the fiery lake of burning sulfur.*
>
> *Revelation 19:20*

Satan will be captured and securely bound and hurled into the Abyss where he will remain for a thousand years.

> *He threw him into the Abyss, and locked and sealed it over him, to keep him from deceiving the nations anymore until the thousand years were ended.*
>
> *Revelation 20:3*

The Greek word *chilia* means 'a thousand', meaning Satan will be in the Abyss for a thousand years.

The armies of Satan will be killed and will go into hades to await the judgement of the great white throne.

> *The angel swung his sickle on the earth, gathered its grapes and threw them into the great winepress of God's wrath. They were trampled in the winepress outside the city, and blood flowed out of the press, rising as high as the horses' bridles for a distance of 1,600 stadia.*
>
> *Revelation 14:19-20*

The harvested grapes refer to all the wicked people on earth who will experience God's wrath as they are crushed like grapes in a winepress.

Their blood will flow for two hundred miles (1,600 stadia) to the depth of the "horses' bridles". This is an awful spectacle, as is the gruesome sight of the birds gorging themselves on the bodies of those killed.

> *The rest were killed with the sword coming out of the mouth of the rider on the horse, and all the birds gorged themselves on their flesh.*
>
> *Revelation 19:21*

Questions

What is the significance of the 'Olivet Discourse' (see p.73)?

_____

_____

_____

_____

Can you identify any other prophesies concerning the Second Coming of Jesus Christ?

_____

_____

_____

_____

_____

Why did the early church believe the return of Jesus Christ would occur in their lifetime?

_____

_____

_____

Why will the Jews be deceived when the Antichrist signs a covenant between Israel and the rest of the world?

_____

_____

_____

What roles do the two beasts play in supporting Satan?

_____

_____

_____

Why does God imprison Satan for a thousand years in the Abyss and not throw him into the fiery lake of burning sulphur with the two beasts?

_____

_____

_____

Interlude

God's planning is thorough and flawless. He does not forget important details even though we often fail to appreciate them. The Second Coming of Jesus Christ follows seven years of Tribulation which will leave the earth in colossal upheaval and utterly devastated. Before Jesus Christ commences his Millennial Reign there is a seventy-five-day interval, or what could be described as a transition period, that follows the end of the second half of the Tribulation period.

> *No account is directly given of that which occupies the interval of seventy-five days between the end of the tribulation and the full blessing of verse 12.*
>
> Rev. C. I. Scofield[44]

According to *Charting the End Times* by Tim LaHaye & Thomas Ice, the changeover from the Tribulation to the glorious millennial kingdom will not be instantaneous. During this time Jesus will ensure the earth is suitable for his millennial rule. There are two consecutive periods of thirty days and forty-five days prophesied by Daniel which the angel "Gabriel" (Dan.10:18, AMP) revealed to him.

> *From the time that the daily sacrifice is abolished and the abomination that causes desolation is set up, there will be 1,290 days. Blessed is the one who waits for and reaches the end of the 1,335 days.*
>
> Daniel 12:11-12

These periods relate to the second half of the Tribulation which commences after 1,260 days when the Antichrist defiles the temple, "ruining the temple for worship of the true God" (Dan.12:11b).

Tim LaHaye and Ed Hindson believe that during the thirty days beyond the 1,260 days (that is, 1260 + 30 = 1,290 days) "the elevation

---

[44] *The Scofield Reference Bible;* p.930; notes 3 & 4

of the millennial Jerusalem will take place and the millennial temple will be built"[45] (see Ez.40-48).

During this period of 75 days the Judgement of the Nations, or the judgement of the sheep and goats, will take place (see Matt.25:31-46), a view shared by John MacArthur.[46]

The angel told Daniel that those who make it to the end of the 75 days period will be "blessed (happy, fortunate, spiritually prosperous) and beloved" (Dan.12:12, AMP).

> *The reason the one who makes it to the end of the 1,335 days is so blessed, is because this will mark the first day of the millennial kingdom and the entrance into it.*
>
> Tim LaHaye & Ed Hindson[47]

> *"Then the King will say to those on his right, 'Come you who are blessed by my Father; take your inheritance, the kingdom prepared for you since the creation of the world.'"*
>
> Matthew 25:34

Whilst these details may seem relatively unimportant in the end-times timetable, it demonstrates God has planned every detail of the transition to the Millennial Reign of Jesus Christ.

---

[45] *The Popular Bible Prophecy Commentary; p.266*
[46] *www.gty.org.library/sermons;* 7 Dec. 1980
[47] *The Popular Bible Prophecy Commentary; p.266*

CHAPTER SIX

Mystery Babylon and Babylon the Great

Introduction

Following the Rapture of the Church, the first beast, known as the Antichrist, will be revealed.

> *The dragon stood on the shore of the sea. And I saw a beast coming out of the sea. It had ten horns and seven heads, with ten crowns on its horns and on each head a blasphemous name. The beast I saw resembled a leopard, but had feet like those of a bear and a mouth like that of a lion. The dragon gave the beast his power and his throne and great authority.*
>
> *Revelation 13:1-2*

The animal symbolism comes from Daniel's prophecy (see Dan.7:4-8) and refers to a time before the Roman Empire was established. The lion represents great power and is a reference to Babylon; whereas the bear signifies ferociousness and is the Medo-Persian empire. The leopard has great speed and refers to Greece which is the empire of Alexander the Great. The dragon, who delegates his power and authority to the Antichrist, is Satan.

The beast coming out of the sea marks the start of the seven-year period of Tribulation. This is when the Antichrist has amassed worldwide power and makes a legal covenant between Israel and the rest of the world.

> *Israel is protected from war by an agreement with the Antichrist, who also permits the rebuilding of the temple in*

Jerusalem and the reinstitution of the sacrificial calendar and services.

Tim LaHaye & Ed Hindson[48]

He will confirm a covenant with many for one 'seven'. In the middle of the 'seven' he will put an end to sacrifice and offering. And at the temple he will set up an abomination that causes desolation, until the end that is decreed is poured out on him.

Daniel 9:27

At the mid-point of the Tribulation (1,260 days), the Antichrist breaks the legal covenant and occupies Jerusalem. He desecrates the temple, stops the practice of sacrifices and offerings, blasphemes God and persecutes the Jews. The False Prophet sets up an image of the Antichrist in the temple and anyone who refuses to worship the Antichrist and acknowledge he is God is "beheaded" (Rev.20:4). This leads to an unprecedented period of persecution against Israel which is when God intensifies his wrath on all unbelievers and demonic forces in the world.

The Second Beast Known as the False Prophet

The Satanic Trinity imitates the godhead and comprises the "dragon" who is Satan, (Rev.13:1) the first "beast coming out of the sea" who is the Antichrist (Rev.13:1b) and the "second beast coming out of the earth" who is the False Prophet (Rev.13:11).

Then I saw a second beast, coming out of the earth. It had two horns like a lamb, but it spoke like a dragon.

Revelation 13:11

The second beast is very powerful and promotes idolatry ruthlessly. It has two horns like a lamb, which are symbols of power and influence, but this is part of his deception. Whilst a lamb appears to be meek and mild, it does not literally have horns. He speaks like a "dragon" because he is Satan's mouthpiece, who is the source of his inspiration and power. Jesus warns us to be on our guard against false prophets and deceptive spirits.

---

[48] *The Popular Bible Prophecy Commentary;* p.235

"Watch out for false prophets. They come to you in sheep's clothing, but inwardly they are ferocious wolves. By their fruit you will recognize them. Do people pick grapes from thornbushes, or figs from thistles?"

Matthew 7:15-16

The apostles warn believers not to be deceived by false spirits and to use the spiritual gift of discernment which is the gift of "distinguishing between spirits" (1.Cor.12:10). Paul says the acid test is, "No one can say 'Jesus is Lord,' except by the Holy Spirit." (1.Cor.12:3)

Dear friends, do not believe every spirit, but test the spirits to see whether they are from God, because many false prophets have gone out into the world. This is how you can recognize the Spirit of God: Every spirit that acknowledges that Jesus Christ has come in the flesh is from God, but every spirit that does not acknowledge Jesus is not from God. This is the spirit of the antichrist, which you have heard is coming and even now is already in the world.

1 John 4:1-3

The second beast or False Prophet exercises vast power because he has delegated authority to act on behalf of the Antichrist and promote the worship of the first beast. The False Prophet is able to deceive unbelievers throughout the world by performing miraculous and satanically inspired signs and wonders that persuade them to worship the Antichrist.

It exercised all the authority of the first beast on its behalf, and made the earth and its inhabitants worship the first beast, whose fatal wound had been healed. And it performed great signs, even causing fire to come down from heaven to the earth in full view of the people. Because of the signs it was given power to perform on behalf of the first beast, it deceived the inhabitants of the earth. It ordered them to set up an image in honor of the beast who was wounded by the sword and yet lived. The second beast was given power to give breath to the image of the first beast, so that the image could speak and cause all who refused to worship the image to be killed.

Revelation 13:12-15

The False Prophet was also given control over all economic activity and made it impossible to buy or sell any goods or services without displaying the mark of the beast.

> *It also forced all people, great and small, rich and poor, free and slave, to receive a mark on their foreheads, so that they could not buy or sell unless they had the mark, which is the name of the beast or the number of its name.*
>
> *Revelation 13:16-17*

History teaches us a flourishing black market would probably emerge as believers realise the implications of taking the mark of the beast. However, it would be very difficult to survive for long without complying with the demands of the False Prophet and his followers. Most of those who accept Jesus Christ as their personal saviour during the Tribulation will end up being beheaded.

The Rise of Mystery Babylon

The False Prophet will set up and lead the false One World Church which is both a religious and political system known as Babylon. In his book *The Two Babylons* by Dr. Alexandra Hislop, published in 1858, he examines the relationship between ancient Babylon and the practices of the harlot system called Mystery Babylon.

> *The name written on her forehead was a mystery:*
> *BABYLON THE GREAT*
> *THE MOTHER OF PROSTITUTES*
> *AND OF THE ABOMINATIONS OF THE EARTH.*
>
> *Revelation 17:5*

The Greek word *musterion* means 'mystery'. The term "abominations" in scripture is another name for idols and idolatrous worship, invariably linked with all kinds of sexual immorality. The history of Babel or Babylon goes back to the reign of Nebuchadnezzar (605-562 B.C.) and to its founder Nimrod.

> *... "Like Nimrod, a mighty hunter before the LORD." The first centers of his kingdom were Babylon, Uruk, Akkad and Kalneh in Shinar.*
>
> *Genesis 10:9b-10*

Nimrod was a ruthless and ambitious warrior whose aim was to rule the world militarily, economically and politically. Nimrod had the ambitious idea to build a city with a tower that would reach up to the heavens which would enormously enhance his reputation.

> "Come let us build ourselves a city, with a tower that reaches to the heavens, so that we may make a name for ourselves; otherwise we will be scattered over the face of the whole earth."
>
> Genesis 11:4

God took great exception to this blatant challenge to his authority and dealt firmly with Nimrod's pride. Confusing the common language everyone used made it impossible for anyone to communicate, and just as Nimrod feared, God scattered everybody throughout the world into different countries where each nation spoke a different language. This meant Nimrod's godless project had to be completely abandoned.

> That is why it was called Babel – because there the LORD confused the language of the whole world.
>
> Genesis 11:9

Nimrod was Noah's great grandson. Noah had three sons: Shem, Japheth and Ham. Ham had four sons: Cush, Egypt, Put and Canaan. Cush was the father of Nimrod, and he "became a mighty warrior on the earth" (Gen.10:8). He was so successful as a commander and warrior that he expanded his kingdom from Babylon, Uruk, Akkad and Kalneh and "he went to Assyria, where he built Ninevah, Rehoboth Ir, Calah and Resen" (Gen.10:11). Nimrod married Semiramis from Ashkelon, whose name means 'highest heaven' and she gave birth to a son they named Tammuz, whom she claimed was miraculously conceived. The people believed he was the promised deliverer and began to worship him as a god.

> Nimrod's wife was the infamous Semiramis the first. She is reputed to have been the founder of the Babylonian mysteries, and the first high priestess of idolatry. Thus Babylon became

the fountainhead of idolatry and the mother of every heathen and pagan system in the world.

Rev. Glyn Taylor[49]

Tammuz was a Phoenician deity, the Adonis of the Greeks. Originally he was a Sumerian or Babylonian sun god, called Dumuzu, the husband of Ishtar who corresponded with the Aphrodite of the Greeks. ... The Babylonian Dunuzu or Tammuz was represented as a beautiful shepherd slain by a wild boar, the symbol of winter. Ishtar long mourned for him and descended into the underworld to deliver him from the embrace of death. ... The death of Tammuz was supposed to typify the long, dry summer of Syria and Palestine, when vegetation perished; and his return to life symbolized the rainy season when the dry land was revived. His death also symbolized the cold, winter season, and his return to life the beautiful and fruitful spring.

Finis Jennings Dake[50]

Ezekiel received a vision from God, in which he was carried away by the Spirit of God to the temple in Jerusalem.

Then he brought me to the entrance of the north gate of the house of the LORD, and I saw women sitting there, mourning the god Tammuz. He said to me, "Do you see this, son of man? You will see things that are even more detestable than this."

Ezekiel 8:14-15

Even worse that the women weeping for Tammuz was the worship of an image of the sun set up by the elders of Israel. They had rejected worshiping God in the Temple's holy of holies and chosen idolatrous sun worship instead.

He then brought me into the inner court of the house of the LORD, and there at the entrance to the temple, between the portico and the altar, were about twenty-five men. With their

---

[49] *One World Religion;* p.8
[50] *Dake's Annotated Reference Bible;* p.812

backs towards the temple of the LORD and their faces towards the east, they were bowing down to the sun in the east.

Ezekiel 8:16

Ezekiel protested against the idolatrous worship of Tammuz but the mysterious cult of the mother and child worship had begun to take hold. This form of idolatry, the oldest form known to man, was a satanic delusion that became popular and well-established. It was normal for idolatry to be accompanied by disgusting and immoral sexual practices.

The image of the 'Queen of Heaven' with a babe in arms was seen throughout the world under the guise of different names. The mother Ashtoreth and child Tammuz of the Phoenicians became Isis and Horus in Egypt, Aphrodite and Eros in Greece, and Venus and Cupid in Italy. The title 'Queen of Heaven' given to Mary by the Roman Catholic Church is used by the prophet Jeremiah to describe the mother of Tammuz, the mother goddess of Babylon, five hundred years before the birth of Jesus Christ. The names Ashtoreth, Queen of Heaven and Ishtar all originate from Babylon – the false religious system.

"We will burn incense to the Queen of Heaven and will pour out drink offerings to her just as we and our ancestors, our kings and our officials did in the towns of Judah and in the streets of Jerusalem."

Jeremiah 44:17b

Within a thousand years Babylonianism had become a world religion and had rejected the divine revelation of Jesus Christ as the promised Messiah. The mystery religion of Babylonianism adopted immoral practices, such as the dedication of virgins to the gods, a form of sanctified prostitution. Other unscriptural practices developed, recognised today by the Roman Catholic Church, including the 'purgatorial purification after death', 'salvation by countless sacraments such as priestly absolution', the practice of 'sprinkling with holy water', 'praying for the dead' and the doctrine of 'transubstantiation'. When we examine the letters to the seven churches, and in particular the church at Thyatira that represents the era of the Papal Church, there is an account of all the unbiblical teaching and doctrines that were adopted by the Roman Catholic Church between 590 and 1517 A.D.

Another infamous Phoenician queen was Jezebel, the daughter of Ethbaal king of the Sidonians, who married King Ahab. She was a devoted Baal worshipper and was instrumental in polluting Judah with Baal worship, which was the Canaanite version of Babylonianism. Jezebel imported nine hundred false prophets into Israel and built a temple complete with an altar to Baal. She ruthlessly promoted Baal worship and proceeded to exterminate most of the Lord's prophets. Things only came to a head when Elijah confronted Ahab and claimed, "You have abandoned the LORD's commands and have followed the Baals." (1.Kgs.18:18) The outcome was a test at Mount Carmel which demonstrated the futility of Baal worship to the people, who turned back to God. As a result, all the prophets of Baal were slaughtered in the Kishon Valley (see 1.Kgs.18:40).

Sometime after the temple was destroyed, the high priests fled with their holy sacred vessels initially to Pergamos (Pergamum) "where Satan has his throne" (Rev.2:13) and then on to Rome which had become the headquarters of Babylonianism. Jeremiah prophesied during the last days of Judah's kingdom the destruction of Babylon, when God decided, "It is time for the LORD's vengeance; he will repay her what she deserves." (Jer.51:6)

> *Babylon will be a heap of ruins,*
> *a haunt of jackals,*
> *an object of horror and scorn,*
> *a place where no one lives.*
>
> *...*
>
> *Her towns will be desolate,*
> *a dry and desert land,*
> *a land where no one lives,*
> *through which no one travels.*
>
> Jeremiah 51:37,43

King Nebuchadnezzar's Dream

In 606 B.C. the Babylonian King Nebuchadnezzar had a troubling dream which none of his magicians and astrologers could recall, let alone interpret (see Dan.2:2).

Daniel, who was renamed Belteshazzar by Nebuchadnezzar after his god (see Dan.4:8), told the king the one true God had revealed the secret dream and its interpretation to him.

"Your Majesty looked, and there before you stood a large statue – an enormous, dazzling statue, awesome in appearance. The head of the statue was made of pure gold, its chest and arms of silver, its belly and thighs of bronze, its legs of iron, its feet partly of iron and partly of baked clay. While you were watching, a rock was cut out, but not by human hands. It struck the statue on its feet of iron and clay and smashed them. Then the iron, the clay, the bronze, the silver and the gold were all broken to pieces and became like chaff on a threshing floor in the summer. The wind swept them away without leaving a trace. But the rock that struck the statue became a huge mountain and filled the whole earth."

Daniel 2:31-35

Daniel proceeded to share the interpretation of the dream, confirming that the head of gold was indeed him.

"Your Majesty, you are the king of kings. The God of heaven has given you dominion and power and might and glory, in your hands he has placed all mankind and the beasts of the field and the birds in the sky. Wherever they live, he has made you ruler over them all. You are that head of gold."

Daniel 2:37-38

The kingdoms that would succeed Nebuchadnezzar's Babylonian empire were represented by silver, bronze and iron – a divided kingdom of iron mixed with clay. The rock that shatters all these kingdoms is the kingdom of God which will smash all these kingdoms in the future and last for all eternity.

"After you, another kingdom will arise, inferior to yours. Next, a third kingdom, one of bronze, will rule over the whole earth. Finally, there will be a fourth kingdom, strong as iron – for iron breaks and smashes everything – and as iron breaks things to pieces, so it will crush and break all the others."

Daniel 2:39-40

The four kingdoms that were prophesied to rule over Israel in the coming centuries were the Babylonian Empire, the Medio-Persian Empire, the Greek Empire and the Roman Empire.

In 555 B.C. during the first year of Belshazzar's reign (Nebuchadnezzar's son), Daniel had another vision where he saw, "Four great beasts, each different from the others, came up out of the sea." (Dan.7:3) These four great beasts were four kings that rose up out from the earth (see Dan.7:17).

The first beast was like a lion with the wings of an eagle, which were torn off and the eagle was lifted off the ground and stood on its feet like a human. The second beast looked like a bear and had three ribs in its mouth between its teeth. The third beast looked like a leopard and had four heads with four wings on its back like a bird. (See Dan.7:4-6.)

The head of "pure gold" represented Nebuchadnezzar's first world empire of Babylon which commenced in 612 B.C. This first beast was "like a lion, and it had the wings of an eagle" (Dan.7:4) which demonstrated the nation would rapidly be united under his rule. The Medes and Persians combined their kingdoms in 550 B.C. under the leadership of King Cyrus and formed the Medo-Persian empire in 538 B.C. after conquering Babylon.

The second beast represented the Medo-Persian empire and "looked like a bear. It was raised up on one of its sides, and it had three ribs in its mouth between its teeth." (Dan.7:5) It was a strong nation militarily with enormous armies of up to 5 million soldiers, well able to overwhelm other nations. The combined forces of Lydia, Babylon and Egypt fought together as allies against Xerxes and Persia's forces but were defeated, as was portrayed as the "three ribs in its mouth between its teeth".

The "chest and arms of silver" (Dan.2:32) represented a united empire comprising of Media (corresponding to the modern regions of Aberbaijan, Kurdistan and parts of Kermanshah) and Persia (which is in southwestern Asia, now modern Iran). "The two-horned ram that you saw represents the kings of Media and Persia. The shaggy goat is the king of Greece, and the large horn between its eyes is the first king." (Dan.8:20-21) The "large horn" represents Media which is larger than Persia. Media and Persia ruled Babylon alternatively until they were defeated and driven out by Alexander the Great of Greece.

The third world empire symbolised by the "belly and thighs of bronze" represents Greece. The third beast was "one that looked like a leopard. And on its back it had four wings like those of a bird. This beast had four heads and was given authority to rule." (Dan.7:6) This meant that due to its swiftness as a leopard with wings it would conquer the whole world with incredible speed, which is what happened. Under

Alexander the Great, the Greek empire expanded enormously and by 330 B.C. encompassed all the known countries in Europe. His empire was so great that it became much bigger than the two preceding Neo-Babylonian and Persian empires. Following the death of Alexander the Great, infighting amongst his generals led to the empire being divided into four parts which comprised Thrace, Macedonia, Egypt and Syria. The Ptolemies were based in Egypt and ruled over Israel. The Seleucids, whose ruler Antiochus IV was based in Syria, imposed Greek culture on Israel.

The fourth world empire is Rome and is represented by two "legs of iron, its feet partly of iron and partly of baked clay" (Dan.2:33). The city of Rome used iron, the strongest of the metals depicted in the vision, to develop weaponry and went on to conquer Greece in 146 B.C. The Roman Empire occupied Israel in 63 B.C. which ended Jewish independence and they destroyed the Jewish temple in A.D. 70, as prophesied by Jesus Christ outside the temple in Jerusalem.

> *"Truly I tell you, not one stone here will be left on another; every one will be thrown down."*
>
> *Matthew 24:2*

By A.D. 395 The Roman Empire had split into two political areas, represented by the two "legs of iron". The West was governed by the Roman church and the East was governed by Constantinople (renamed in 1930 as Istanbul in Turkey) and known nowadays as the Greek Orthodox Church.

Daniel reveals the fourth beast was a horrifying and very powerful monster that represents the expanding Roman Empire. Daniel saw the ten horns as a league of ten nations ruled by ten kings who receive their authority from the fourth beast, who is the Antichrist.

> *"I looked, and there before me was a fourth beast – terrifying and frightening and very powerful. It had large iron teeth; it crushed and devoured its victims and trampled underfoot whatever was left. It was different from all the former beasts, and it had ten horns. While I was thinking about the horns, there before me was another horn, a little one, which came up among them; and three of the first horns were uprooted before it. This horn had eyes like the eyes of a human being and a mouth that spoke boastfully."*
>
> *Daniel 7:7-8*

103

The word *qeren* in Aramaic means 'horn' and depicts power or authority. The "horn, a little one" which subdued "three of the first horns" represents the Antichrist who will dominate the whole world during the Great Tribulation and oppose God. However, Satan's time of domination of the world using the Antichrist and the False Prophet will be short-lived, because the Lord Jesus Christ is going to return like a rock and smash their kingdom to pieces.

> *"But the rock that struck the statue became a huge mountain that filled the whole earth."*
>
> *Daniel 2:35*

This means that when Jesus Christ intervenes, represented by the mountain, he will remove all human governments and establish the kingdom of God. This is the fifth kingdom which occurs during the seventieth week of Daniel's prophecy and differs from the previous kingdoms as it is a divine kingdom set up by Jesus Christ when he establishes the eternal millennial kingdom.

> *"In the time of those kings, the God of heaven will set up a kingdom that will never be destroyed, nor will it be left to another people. It will crush all those kingdoms and bring them to an end, but it will itself endure forever."*
>
> *Daniel 2:44*

It is interesting to note that the founders of the European Union based their design for the Strasbourg Parliament on the unfinished 'Tower of Babel' by renaissance painter Peter Bruegel. The 'Woman on the Beast' sculpture is also the main feature outside the front of the building of the Council of Ministers in Europe and represents the Greek myth of the 'Rape of Europa'. The forehead of this sculpture has a second name, Mystery Babylon.

Mystery Babylon is Established

In *One World Religion* by Rev. Glyn Taylor, he describes how Rome became significant in the development of Babylonianism.

> *When the city and temples of Babylon were destroyed, the high priest and associates fled with their sacred vessels firstly to Pergamos and then to Rome which became the headquarters of Babylonianism.*

Once the priests had established themselves in Rome, the chief priest took the title *'Pontifex Maximus'*, meaning 'Supreme Priest'. When Julius Caesar became head of state he was elected *'Pontifex Maximus'*, a title held by all Roman Emperors down to Constantine the Great, who became both Head of the Church to Christians and High Priest to the pagans.

The Roman Catholic Church unofficially came into being in 312 A.D. when Constantine had a miraculous conversion to Christianity – supposedly, because he still worshipped the pagan sun god! From 312 A.D. until his death in 337 A.D. Constantine was involved in simultaneously building pagan temples and Christian churches, then he slowly transferred control of this pagan priesthood together with the title *'Pontifex Maximus'* or 'Bishop of Rome' to the Pope, a title used by the head of the Roman Catholic Church today.

The false doctrines and practices adopted by Romanism can be traced back to the time paganism was combined with Christianity and Constantine declared Rome to be the centre of Christianity. This led to huge compromises with biblical teaching and the introduction of practices that are unscriptural. One example is that successive popes believe they are Jesus Christ's representatives on earth and are infallible; but only Jesus Christ demonstrated he was sinless.

> *But we have one who has been tempted in every way, just as we are – yet he did not sin.*
>
> *Hebrews 4:15b*

However, subsequent popes have demonstrated their fallibility by leading flawed and unrighteous lives. The immorality of Rome was so widespread that Martin Luther said, "If there be hell, Rome is built over it." Although pagan popes can be traced back to Babylon, no Christian popes held that office until Constantine declared himself to be Pope in 312 A.D.

The apostle John became an eye-witness to the religious system represented by the great prostitute, that is Mystery Babylon.

> *One of the seven angels who had the seven bowls came and said to me, "Come I will show you the punishment of the great prostitute who sits by many waters."*
>
> *Revelation 17:1*

105

The reference to "many waters" concerns the vastness of the nations of the earth: the "peoples, multitudes, nations and languages" (Rev.17:15).

> *"With her the kings of the earth committed adultery, and the inhabitants of the earth were intoxicated with the wine of her adulteries."*
>
> *Revelation 17:2*

The punishment of Babylon, which is the great prostitute (the Greek word *porne* means 'whore') and is "the great city that rules over the kings of the earth" (Rev.17:18), will be at the hands of the Antichrist and the ten nations who "will bring her to ruin and leave her naked; they will eat her flesh and burn her with fire" (Rev.17:16).

John is then taken into the wilderness and sees the religious system Mystery Babylon in all its finery with her disgusting mystery name written across her forehead:

> *BABYLON THE GREAT*
> *THE MOTHER OF PROSTITUTES*
> *AND THE ABOMINATIONS OF THE EARTH.*
>
> *Revelation 17:5*

> *I saw a woman sitting on a scarlet beast that was covered in blasphemous names and had <u>seven heads</u> and <u>ten horns</u>. The woman was dressed in purple and scarlet, and was glittering with <u>gold, precious stones and pearls</u>. She held a <u>golden cup</u> in her hand, filled with abominable things and the filth of her adulteries.*
>
> *Revelation 17:3-4 (emphasis added)*

Her "gold, precious stones and pearls" are used ruthlessly by her to persuade the kings of the earth to do her bidding, whilst the "golden cup" represents the immoral and disgraceful sinful acts which she performed. The "ten horns" are ten kings who formed a coalition of ten Gentile nations and the "seven heads" are the rulers who govern these ten countries under the leadership of the beast. Their aim is to form a powerful and resurgent Roman Empire under the direction of the Antichrist.

> *"The ten horns are ten kings who will come from this kingdom. After them another king will arise, different from the earlier ones; he will subdue three kings."*
>
> Daniel 7:24

The religious system that is Babylon, is hungry for power and willingly exchanges sexual favours for power and influence. She lives in great majesty like a queen and dresses seductively in fine clothing to charm and seduce the world with her evil practices. There is a sinister and bloodthirsty side to this Mystery Babylon as it persecutes and kills believers, a fact John finds astonishing.

> *I saw that the woman was drunk with the blood of God's holy people, the blood of those who bore testimony to Jesus.*
>
> Revelation 17:6

John finds it incredulous to learn the 'One World Church' of end times is so evil, duplicitous and blood-thirsty that it gets great satisfaction from persecuting and murdering believers. The angel tells John not to be "astonished" (Rev.17:7) and proceeds to explain "the mystery of the woman and of the beast she rides, which has the seven heads and ten horns" (Rev.17:7).

> *"The beast, which you saw, once was, now is not, and yet will come up out of the Abyss and go to its destruction. The inhabitants of the earth whose names have not been written in the book of life from the creation of the world will be astonished when they see the beast, because it once was, now is not, and yet will come."*
>
> Revelation 17:8

This relates to the first beast the Antichrist, who suffers the deadly wound and recovers. This deception astonishes the whole world of unbelievers who swallow his lies, but we learn his future punishment is assured and both beasts will be "thrown alive into the fiery lake of burning sulfur" (Rev.19:20).

The angel also explains to John that "the seven heads are seven hills on which the woman sits" (Rev.17:9). The expression "heads" often means rulers or kings in scripture. Some scholars believe the seven hills are the seven hills of Rome: the Capitoline, Palatine, Aventine, Viminal, Quirinal, Esquiline and Caelian.

"There are also seven kings. Five have fallen, one is, the other has not yet come; but when he does come, he must remain for only a little while. The beast who once was, and now is not, is an eighth king. He belongs to the seven and is going to his destruction."

Revelation 17:10-11

The beast would be one of the seven kings in his kingdom, but then the eighth king is seen to be the ruler who received the deadly wound and then comes up out of the Abyss. When this takes place he becomes the eighth king. This eighth king will be a world dictator who receives supernatural powers when he is 'revived' by Satan. Making the eighth king identical to the beast out of the Abyss seems to be the only interpretation that makes sense.

Tim LaHaye & Ed Hindson[51]

The Antichrist is clearly the eighth king, who subdues three of the nations and becomes the eighth king.

"The ten horns you saw are ten kings who have not yet received a kingdom, but who for one hour will receive authority as kings along with the beast."

Revelation 17:12

The ten nations have one purpose in mind, which is to wage war against Jesus Christ and his believers. They promise their allegiance to the beast during the second half of the Tribulation (1,260 days) until they have fought against Jesus Christ and his army of believers in the Valley of Megiddo.

Mystery Babylon is Destroyed

The Antichrist allows the 'One World Church' to temper his actions during the first 1,260 days of the Tribulation. During this time, he builds his power base amongst the nations of the world and becomes very powerful. In the meantime, the religious system of Babylon has become too influential and has reached a point where "the woman you saw is the great city that rules over the kings of the earth" (Rev.17:18). The extent

---

[51] *The Popular Bible Prophecy Commentary;* p.533

of power the prostitute woman Babylon wields alienates the coalition of ten nations. So, in the middle of the Tribulation the Antichrist throws caution to the wind, breaks the peace treaty and flexes his muscles. His true nature as a ruthless and autocratic leader becomes apparent. Acting in consort with the ten kings, the Antichrist completely destroys and humiliates the prostitute Babylon.

> *"The beast and the ten horns you saw will hate the prostitute. They will bring her to ruin and leave her naked: they will eat her flesh and burn her with fire."*
>
> *Revelation 17:16*

The ten powers ('horns') and the beast turn against the Mystery Babylon and confiscate her temples and huge stores of gold.

> *"God has put it into their hearts to accomplish his purpose by agreeing to hand over to the beast their royal authority, until God's words are fulfilled."*
>
> *Revelation 17:17*

God influences the godless nations to accomplish his divine purpose, and the nations acting out of selfish motives and greed proceed to destroy the corrupt and immoral Babylonian religious system once and for all.

Now that the world is unable to worship the Mystery Babylonian religion, the False Prophet sets up an image of the Antichrist in the temple and forces everyone to worship him as God. Having earlier deceived everyone with "great signs, even causing fire to come down from heaven to the earth in full view of the people" (Rev.13:13), all the unbelievers are impressed and "the whole world was filled with wonder and followed the beast" (Rev.13:3b).

Babylon the Great is Destroyed

The destruction of the Mystery Babylon in the middle of the Tribulation is a major evil that has been purged from the earth and causes great rejoicing in heaven. The destruction of the city of Babylon does not finally occur until the end of the Great Tribulation, when it experiences God's cataclysmic judgement.

The apostle John sees a powerful angel coming down from heaven whose splendour is so magnificent that it illuminates the earth and makes this triumphant announcement in a thunderous voice:

> *"'Fallen! Fallen is Babylon the Great!' She has become a dwelling for demons and a haunt for every impure spirit, a haunt for every unclean bird, a haunt for every unclean and detestable animal. For all the nations have drunk the maddening wine of her adulteries. The kings of the earth committed adultery with her, and the merchants of the earth grew rich from her excessive luxuries."*
>
> *Revelation 18:2-3*

The Greek words *akathartos* and *pneuma* mean 'impure' and 'spirit'. This refers to the corrupt nature of Satan's demons that tempt people to indulge in the most evil and immoral of practices. Babylon has become so evil and corrupt that it has become far worse than Sodom and Gomorrah. The citizens are warned to escape from Babylon and not to indulge in her sinful practices, otherwise they will be judged along with the city and suffer plagues, famine, fire and death.

> *"Therefore in one day her plagues will overtake her: death, mourning and famine. She will be consumed by fire, for mighty is the Lord God who judges her."*
>
> *Revelation 18:8*

The lavish trade which has enabled merchants, businessmen and bankers to grow rich will cause enormous consternation and distress as their lucrative trade suddenly collapses. Many vile and evil practices also cease like "human beings sold as slaves" (Rev.18:13b).

> *When they see the smoke of her burning, they will exclaim,* "Was there ever a city like this great city?"
>
> *Revelation 18:18*

Judgement on the city of Babylon will be brutal and violent.

> *"In one hour she has been brought to ruin."*
>
> *Revelation 18:19b*

> *Then a mighty angel picked up a boulder the size of a large millstone and threw it into the sea, and said:* "With such violence the great city of Babylon will be thrown down, never to be found again."
>
> *Revelation 18:21*

Never again will there be the sound of musicians, or any trade, industry or work carried out in the city. Never again will any lights shine, no couples will ever get married in the city nor will any important businessmen come to stay. The city of Babylon has been such a corrupting force that it has led astray the population of the world and been responsible for the deaths of many followers of Jesus Christ (see Rev.18:22-24).

> *"Salvation and glory and power belong to our God,*
> *for true and just are his judgments.*
> *He has condemned the great prostitute*
> *who corrupted the earth by her adulteries.*
> *He has avenged on her the blood of his servants."*
> *And again they shouted:*
> *"Hallelujah!*
> *The smoke from her goes up for ever and ever."*
>
> *Revelation 19:2-3*

This rejoicing anticipates "the wedding supper of the Lamb" (Rev.19:9) which is when believers, who are the bride of Jesus Christ, return to earth with him.

Points for Reflection

The One World false religion prompts the question, "What is spiritual prostitution?" God gives several examples from scripture of what he considers to be spiritual prostitution.

- Don't break your agreement with God by worshipping other gods.

> *"...these people will soon prostitute themselves to the foreign gods."*
>
> *Deuteronomy 31:16*

- Be careful of the company you choose to worship with.

> *"...when they prostitute themselves to their gods and sacrifice to them, they will invite you and you will eat their sacrifices."*
>
> *Exodus 34:15*

- Don't eat food sacrificed to idols or be sexually immoral.

"You are to abstain from food sacrificed to idols … and from sexual immorality."

Acts 15:29

- Don't bring tithes and offerings to God from immoral earnings.

You must not bring the earnings of a female prostitute or of a male prostitute into the house of the LORD.

Deuteronomy 23:18

- Be righteous and do not compromise your integrity.

See how the faithful city
  has become a prostitute!

…

Your rulers are rebels,
  partners with thieves;
they all love bribes
  and chase after gifts.

Isaiah 1:21,23

- Believers have a responsibility to serve the Lord.

"Long ago you broke off your yoke
  and tore off your bonds;
  you said, 'I will not serve you!'"

Jeremiah 2:20a

- Be wary of giving priority to creating a good image.

"But you trusted in your beauty and used your fame to become a prostitute."

Ezekiel 16:15

- Always put God first in your life.

You adulterous people, don't you know that friendship with the world means enmity against God? Therefore, anyone who chooses to be a friend of the world becomes an enemy of God.

James 4:4

Questions

Why should believers be wary of the 'World Council of Churches' and the ecumenical movement?

_____

_____

_____

How can believers avoid being deceived by false prophets and teachers?

_____

_____

_____

_____

Is the Roman Catholic Church represented by the "woman and of the beast she rides" (Rev.17:7)?

_____

_____

Could the worldwide church be the Roman Catholic Church or Islam, as some scholars think?

_____

_____

Could the False Prophet with "two horns" (Rev.13:11) represent a false worldwide church of 'Chrislam', which is a combination of Christianity and Islam?

_____

_____

Is there any evidence to indicate the European Union has a role in prophetic events?

_____

_____

_____

_____

CHAPTER SEVEN

The Millennial Reign of Jesus Christ

Introduction

We have covered the Rapture, the time of Tribulation and the Second Coming of Jesus Christ and seen how the Antichrist and the False Prophet will be defeated and "thrown alive into the fiery lake of burning sulfur"(Rev.19:20) and also how Satan will be banished to the Abyss for a thousand years.

We have examined how the false worldwide religion of Mystery Babylon will be destroyed and the city called Babylon the Great will be violently reduced to ruin in one hour and will never again be restored.

The coming of Jesus Christ in his Glorious Appearing with all believers will usher in the millennial kingdom – the righteous reign of Jesus Christ on earth.

The Power and Authority of Jesus Christ

During the Millennial Reign of Jesus Christ, he will literally rule the world from Jerusalem. This will be the time when he answers our prayers that God's will is done on earth as it is in heaven, because only righteous persons will be admitted to his kingdom.

> *"'Our Father in heaven,*
> *hallowed be your name,*
> *your kingdom come,*
> *your will be done,*
> *on earth as it is in heaven.'"*

Matthew 6:9-10

This will be an astonishing time for all those alive during this thousand-year period because Jesus Christ will demonstrate that when the earth is governed according to God's laws, the experience will transform our enjoyment of life under his just and righteous rule.

115

The LORD will be king over the whole earth. On that day there
will be one LORD, and his name the only name.

Zechariah 14:9

Therefore God exalted him to the highest place and gave him
the name that is above every name, that at the name of Jesus
every knee should bow, in heaven and on earth and under the
earth, and every tongue acknowledge that Jesus Christ is Lord,
to the glory of God the Father.

Philippians 2:9-11

God will order affairs through his son Jesus Christ, who will have full executive and delegated authority to rule on behalf of God. The Millennium will be a time when he will rule the nations with righteousness and no wickedness will be tolerated.

"Before me every knee will bow;
* by me every tongue will swear.*
They will say of me, 'In the LORD alone
* are deliverance and strength.'"*

Isaiah 45:23b-24a

His kingdom will be a 'theocracy' and God will be recognised as the supreme civil ruler. God will be ordering affairs through his wise and holy son Jesus Christ. His perfect rule will correct all the mistakes of our imperfect governments and address the injustices in our society and criminal justice system.

"He will rule them with an iron scepter."

Revelation 19:15

When the Lord sets up His kingdom, there will be no Sikhs, Muslims, Hindus, atheists or any other cults – only believers (see Matt.25:31-46).

"He will separate the people from one another as a shepherd
separates the sheep from the goats. He will put the sheep on
his right and the goats on his left."

Matthew 25:32b-33

No criminal activity will be tolerated, so there will be no need for police, prison staff or probation officers. The present inequalities in the world will be addressed, where political power is misused and resources are exploited for the benefit of powerful countries. No longer will the abuse of power be allowed or discrimination on the grounds of gender, race, colour or social class be permitted.

For God does not show favoritism.

Romans 2:11

Many people will come and say, "Come, let us go up to the mountain of the LORD, to the temple of the God of Jacob. He will teach us his ways, so that we may walk in his paths." The law will go out from Zion, the word of the LORD from Jerusalem.

Isaiah 2:3

Jesus Christ will rule with great authority and power. Righteousness, justice, truth and holiness will be the values that govern society for evermore. Everyone will respect, honour and benefit from following the commandments of God – which is how God intended his creation to work together in harmony.

The Peaceful Reign of Jesus Christ

During the Millennial Reign there will be no wars or conflict anywhere in the world. In the past 5,000 years it is estimated that there have been less than 300 days when there has not been a serious conflict taking place anywhere in the world. Under the rule of Jesus Christ, peace will become so normal that mankind will forget how to wage war. The whole massive industry of manufacturing armaments and training military personnel will become redundant. All those resources will be freed up to be channelled into productive peaceful activity.

He will judge between the nations
and will settle disputes for many peoples.
They will beat their swords into plowshares
and their spears into pruning hooks.
Nation will not take up sword against nation,
nor will they train for war anymore.

Isaiah 2:4

Peace will extend to the animal kingdom, and wild animals will be docile and live alongside species they would normally hunt and kill. Even dangerous animals that pose a lethal threat to a toddler will be completely harmless. Toddlers and young children will play with complete safety in close proximity to a "cobra", one of the most dangerous snakes in the world, or the "viper", another venomous snake from the *Viperidae* family of snakes – which includes adders, pit vipers, rattlesnakes, copper-mouths and copperheads.

> *The wolf will live with the lamb,*
> *the leopard will lie down with the goat,*
> *the calf and the lion and the yearling together;*
> *and a little child will lead them.*
> *The cow will feed with the bear,*
> *their young will lie down together,*
> *and the lion will eat straw like the ox.*
> *The infant will play near the cobra's den,*
> *and the young child will put its hand into the viper's nest.*
>
> Isaiah 11:6-8

There will be no rebellion whilst Satan is in the Abyss. No one will set up false images and worship idols, or practice witchcraft, or worship the occult and other ungodly practices. Nobody "blasphemes against the Holy Spirit" (Mk.3:29) or expresses "proud words and blasphemies" (Rev.13:5).

> *"For rebellion is as (serious as) the sin of divination (fortune-telling),*
> *And disobedience is as (serious as) false religion and idolatry."*
>
> 1 Samuel 15:23 (AMP)

However, we are warned the seeds of rebellion will be there; for instance, there will be a requirement that all the nations celebrate the Feast of Tabernacles each year, and...

> *If any of the families of the earth do not go up to Jerusalem to worship the King, the Lord of hosts, there will be no rain upon them.*
>
> Zechariah 14:17 (NRSV)

Jesus Christ will break the nations with a "rod of iron" (Ps.2:9) and rule the nations "with an iron scepter" (Rev.19:15) to ensure his perfect divine rule continues.

Habakkuk prophesied spiritual knowledge and understanding will greatly increase.

For the earth will be filled with the knowledge of the glory of the LORD
   as the waters cover the sea.

Habakkuk 2:14

Everyone, including the wild animals and snakes, will know that Jesus Christ is the ruler of the world until the thousand years are over.

The fruit of that righteousness will be peace;
   its effect will be quietness and confidence forever.
My people will live in peaceful dwelling places,
   in secure homes,
   in undisturbed places of rest.

Isaiah 32:17-18

Immortal Bodies

Those who return with Christ during the Millennium will have immortal bodies that are not subject to natural laws, so they will not grow older or deteriorate and become feeble over time. Raptured believers will have their perishable bodies transformed "in a flash, in the twinkling of an eye" (1.Cor.15:52) to immortal bodies. Our bodies will be perfectly restored and they will be like that of the Lord Jesus Christ after he was gloriously resurrected – perfectly formed and looking like we are in the prime of life.

And we eagerly await a Savior from there, the Lord Jesus Christ, who by the power that enables him to bring everything under his control, will transform our lowly bodies so that they will be like his glorious body.

Philippians 3:20-21

There will no sickness or health issues and no need for doctors, nurses or surgeons, because all believers will have immortal bodies. All those who live through the Tribulation or are born during the Millennium, will live longer, healthier lives.

Just as we have borne the image of the earthly [the man of dust], we will also bear the image of the heavenly [the Man of heaven].

1 Corinthians 15:49 (AMP)

Quality of Life

Nobody who is not a believer will enter the Millennium. Those born during the Millennium will have normal perishable bodies but will enjoy long, healthy lives. This was normal in the time period between Adam and Noah – "Methuselah lived a total of 969 years" (Gen.5:27).

There will be no infant mortality in the Millennium, and longevity will be restored. Everyone will reach a certain age, because those who only attain the age of one hundred years old will be considered to be thought of as a "mere child" – the implication being that a normal life span might be several hundred years.

> *"Never again will there be in it*
> *an infant who lives but a few days,*
> *or an old man who does not live out his years;*
> *the one who dies at a hundred*
> *will be thought a mere child;*
> *the one who fails to reach a hundred*
> *will be considered accursed."*
>
>

Isaiah 65:20

There will be every opportunity for those born during the Millennium to receive Jesus Christ as their personal saviour.

> *Those who die at the age of 100 evidently are sinners (unbelievers), for only they would be considered accursed.*
>
>

Tim LaHaye & Ed Hindson[52]

People will have productive and satisfying work to undertake. The houses they build will not suffer from maintenance problems or deteriorate over time or need constant painting. They will live in a clean, wholesome environment; their gardens and orchards will be fertile and weed-free, so everything planted will germinate and give back a fruitful harvest.

> *They will build houses and dwell in them;*
> *they will plant vineyards and eat their fruit.*
> *No longer will they build houses and others live in them,*
> *or plant and others eat.*
> *For as the days of a tree,*

---

[52] *The Popular Bible Prophecy Commentary; p.148*

so will be the days of my people;
  my chosen ones will long enjoy
  the work of their hands.

Isaiah 65:21-22

No one will suffer injury due to an accident and die prematurely. There will be no sorrow and unhappiness as children fail to thrive or are born with disabilities like those caused by Thalidomide, due to mankind's well-meaning ignorance. There will be no birth defects caused by a mother taking medication or becoming addicted to drugs or suffering from excessive consumption of alcohol (foetal alcohol syndrome) at critical points in the pregnancy. The heartbreaking abortion of babies will cease; no women will have a miscarriage or endure painful deliveries. No child will be born with special needs that prevent them achieving their full potential. Everything will be restored to how God intended things should be, with every child being a blessing to their parents and being cared for lovingly, so they achieve their full potential. No abuse, exploitation or non-accidental injury to a child will occur; they will all have the opportunity to lead productive lives.

They will not labor in vain,
  nor will they bear children doomed to misfortune;
for they will be a people blessed by the LORD,
  they and their descendants with them.

Isaiah 65:23

Intellectual capacity will increase, and this greater knowledge and understanding of environmental issues, biology, science and art will enable us to appreciate God's magnificent creation and enhance our ability to worship him and understand his character. Whilst knowledge will increase, this will not be the head knowledge and capacity to remember facts and figures that makes people proud, but the ability to appreciate the glory of God and learn from his infinite wisdom and goodness.

"Has not the LORD Almighty determined
  that the people's labor is only fuel for the fire,
  that the nations exhaust themselves for nothing?
For the earth will be filled with the knowledge of the glory of
the LORD

as the waters cover the sea. "

Habakkuk 2:13-14

Jesus Christ will clean up the environment and restore the beauty and wholesome nature of the oceans and the corals and sea-life to a perfect state.

> *"This water flows toward the eastern region and goes down into the Arabah, where it enters the Dead Sea. When it empties into the sea, the salty waters there become fresh."*

Ezekiel 47:8

The Dead Sea contains a cocktail of chemicals which have a cleansing effect on natural life and result in restoration. The Dead Sea contains ten times more minerals than normal sea salt and includes minerals such as magnesium, calcium, zinc, potassium and sulphur which have fantastic health, therapeutic and detoxifying properties.

The Millennial Reign

In the government of Jesus Christ will be all those believers of the First Resurrection who returned to earth at his Second Coming. All resurrected believers will have important responsibilities and roles in Jesus Christ's kingdom. The twelve disciples have already been allocated their role in the millennial kingdom, which is to govern the twelve Jewish tribes which comprise Israel.

> *Jesus said to them, "Truly I tell you, at the renewal of all things, when the Son of Man sits on his glorious throne, you who have followed me will also sit on twelve thrones, judging the twelve tribes of Israel."*

Matthew 19:28

At the "first resurrection" (Rev.20:6a) all those martyrs beheaded by the Antichrist's cohorts during the Tribulation, for being witnesses to the gospel of Jesus Christ and refusing to take the mark of the beast, will come to life and reign with Jesus Christ for a thousand years.

> *I saw thrones on which were seated those who had been given authority to judge. And I saw the souls of those who had been beheaded because of their testimony about Jesus and because of the word of God. They had not worshipped the beast or its image and had not received its mark on their foreheads or their*

hands. They came to life and reigned with Christ a thousand
years.

Revelation 20:4

Prosperity

The greed and selfishness that allowed half the world to be short of food, due to man's wickedness and defects in our capitalist, materialistic systems, will be corrected under his perfect rule. There will be no poverty or famine anymore because food will be plentiful. Everything will grow without the need for fertilisers; the fields and deserts will both be fertile and yield huge quantities of produce.

> *...the desert becomes a fertile field,*
> *   and the fertile field seems like a forest.*
> *The LORD's justice will dwell in the desert,*
> *   his righteousness live in the fertile field.*

Isaiah 32:15-16

There will be no problems of distributing food as everyone will have more than sufficient for their needs. Everything will be restored to how God intended creation to be before sin entered the world.

> *The desert and the parched land will be glad;*
> *   the wilderness will rejoice and blossom.*
> *Like the crocus it will burst into bloom;*
> *   it will rejoice greatly and shout for joy.*

Isaiah 35:1-2

There is a caveat applicable to any disobedient nations that refuse to go up to Jerusalem to celebrate the Feast of Tabernacles. They will be punished by God and "they will have no rain" (Zech.14:17). The plague and punishment referred to (Zech.14:18-19) is generally accepted as being hunger or famine.

Israel's Pre-eminence

God will elevate Israel to her proper place and restore the Jews to their homeland, who will become a blessing to all the other nations. Israel is God's chosen nation and he promised Abraham that the land of Israel would be their home forever. The Jews have been blessed with natural abilities in technological, medical, scientific, artistic and entrepreneurial expertise.

Despite the destruction that has been inflicted on Jerusalem, its temple and God's holy city, the city will be rebuilt and become so magnificent that all the world will be astonished at its unsurpassed beauty and want to know more about God.

Every Jew throughout the world will be brought back to their homeland from every country throughout the world. God will restore them by giving them a new heart and love for the things of God, as the prophet Ezekiel prophesied.

> *"I will give them an undivided heart and put a new spirit in them; I will remove from them their heart of stone and give them a heart of flesh."*
>
> *Ezekiel 11:19*

Although God will bring his people out of all the countries where they have been scattered, only those who have been born again will enter the land of Israel and the Millennium. No rebellious and unrepentant Jews will be allowed to enter the Kingdom.

In the parable of 'The Sheep and the Goats' Jesus made it clear that when he returns in all his glory and sits on his throne he will separate the righteous people from the unrighteous "as a shepherd separates the sheep from the goats" (Matt.25:32b). He will put the sheep on his right hand and the goats on his left.

> *"The King will say to those on his right, 'Come, you who are blessed by my Father; take your inheritance, the kingdom prepared for you since the creation of the world.'"*
>
> *Matthew 25:34*

The unrighteous "will go away to eternal punishment, but the righteous to eternal life" (Matt.25:46). The lesson is similar to the parable of 'The Wise and Foolish Virgins' at the Galilean wedding banquet who were refused entry because of their foolishness: "And the door was shut." (Matt.25:10)

> *"I will bring you from the nations and gather you from the countries where you have been scattered – with a mighty hand and an outreached arm and with outpoured wrath. I will bring you into the wilderness of the nations and there, face to face,*

I will execute judgment upon you. As I judge your ancestors in the wilderness of the land of Egypt, so I will judge you, declares the Sovereign LORD. I will take note of you as you pass under my rod, and I will bring you into the bond of the covenant. I will purge you of those who revolt and rebel against me. Although I will bring them out of the land where they are living, yet they will not enter the land of Israel."

Ezekiel 20:34-38

The Jews will finally realise that Jesus is their true Messiah and that they were blinkered and deceived in the past. They will regret the dreadful mistake they made of rejecting him when he first came to earth. Their distress and regret will be so enormous that it will be comparable to the weeping and wailing that follows the slaughter following the Battle of Armageddon, when millions were slaughtered on the plain of Megiddo.

"They will mourn for him as one mourns for an only child, and grieve bitterly for him as one grieves for a firstborn son. On that day the weeping in Jerusalem will be as great as the weeping of Hadad Rimmon in the plain of Megiddo. The land will mourn, each clan by itself, with their wives by themselves."

Zechariah 12:10-12

God has no intention of punishing the Jews for past mistakes but to bring the nation into repentance and ensure they permanently cease being unfaithful and worshipping false gods. God intends to establish a new covenant with His chosen nation and will ensure they do not disobey God's laws because the laws will be constantly on their mind.

*"This is the covenant I will make with the people of Israel
    after that time," declares the LORD.
"I will put my law in their minds
    and write it on their hearts.
I will be their God,
    and they will be my people."*

Jeremiah 31:33

Those who return to Israel will have a new resolve to please God and become a blessing to all the nations, as was God's original intention.

"The children of your oppressors will come bowing before you;
all who despise you will bow down at your feet
and will call you the city of the LORD,
Zion of the Holy One of Israel."

Isaiah 60:14

The country will prosper as the world recognises Jesus Christ is blessing the Jewish nation. "How much greater riches will their full inclusion bring" (Rom.11:12) when their talents are fully utilised for the benefit of all mankind. There will be a complete reversal in the fortunes of the nation of Israel. The nations of the world will become deferential to them when they enter the holy city of Jerusalem to worship God.

And I saw the glory of the God of Israel coming from the east.
His voice was like the roar of rushing waters, and the land was
radiant with his glory. The vision I saw was like the vision I
had seen when he came to destroy the city and like the visions
I had seen by the Kebar River, and I fell facedown.

Ezekiel 43:2-3

The Kebar River (translated as the "river Chebar" in the KJV) was a river of Mesopotamia in the land of the Chaldeans, which is mostly in Iraq and Kuwait but also in East Syria and South East Turkey.

The Feast of Tabernacles

In the Millennium Israel will become the most important country in the world, and Jerusalem the most important city. Jesus will be King of the Jews and the world will be governed from Jerusalem. It will be a land that is bountiful, prosperous and environmentally clean and pure. Although the city of Jerusalem has known much strife, unhappiness and heartache over the centuries, God has different ideas for its future.

"But be glad and rejoice forever
in what I will create,
for I will create Jerusalem to be a delight
and its people a joy.
I will rejoice over Jerusalem
and take delight in my people..."

Isaiah 65:18-19

There will be a new zeal to serve God, to obey his commandments and honour his holy name. They will acknowledge and appreciate that Jesus Christ has saved sinners from the judgement they deserve.

> *"At that time they will call Jerusalem The Throne of the LORD, and all nations will gather in Jerusalem to honor the name of the LORD."*
>
> Jeremiah 3:17

Everyone will bow the knee to Jesus Christ and acknowledge that He is Lord. The religious festivals of Israel will be respected and observed by every country in the world and they will be obliged to make an annual pilgrimage to Jerusalem to observe the Feast of Tabernacles.

> *Look on Zion, the city of our festivals;*
> *your eyes will see Jerusalem,*
> *a peaceful abode, a tent that will not be moved;*
> *its stakes will never be pulled up,*
> *nor any of its ropes broken.*
> *There the LORD will be our Mighty One.*
>
> Isaiah 33:20-21a

The Feast of Tabernacles (*Sukkot* in Hebrew) is a Jewish celebration that takes place on the fifteenth day of the seventh month, which is the Hebrew month of Tishri, and lasts for seven days. It was a celebration of thanks to God for bringing them out of captivity and slavery in Egypt. Many theologians see this feast as symbolic of the Second Coming of Jesus Christ when he establishes his earthly kingdom. This celebration, known as the Feast of Tabernacles, or Shelters, or Booths, was a requirement of the Jewish nation, and they built temporary shelters in which to camp out the week and eat their meals in their *sukka*.[53]

> *"Celebrate the Festival of Tabernacles for seven days after you have gathered the produce of your threshing floor and your winepress. Be joyful at your festival – you, your sons and daughters, your male and female servants, and the Levites, the foreigners, the fatherless and the widows who live in your towns. For seven days celebrate the festival to the LORD your God at the place the LORD will choose. For the LORD your*

---

[53] *Strong's Exhaustive Concordance of the Bible;* p.1545

127

God will bless you in all your harvest and in the work of your hands, and your joy will be complete."

Deuteronomy 16:13-15

The kingdom that Jesus Christ sets up will be holy and observe all God's laws. Any nation that does not come to Jerusalem to celebrate the Festival of Tabernacles each year will be punished and that country will experience drought and famine.

> *Then the survivors from all the nations that have attacked Jerusalem will go up year by year to worship the King, the LORD Almighty, and to celebrate the Feast of Tabernacles. If any of the peoples of the earth do not go up to Jerusalem to worship the King, the LORD Almighty, they will have no rain. If the Egyptian people do not go up and take part, they will have no rain. The LORD will bring on them the plague he inflicts on the nations that do not go up to celebrate the Festival of Tabernacles.*

Zechariah 14:16-18

Jesus Christ is determined that all people will worship God, observe his holy festivals and realise Israel and the Jews are a holy and special nation.

Questions

Will children born during the Millennium be able to exercise free will or is this only possible after Satan is released from the Abyss?

_____

_____

Will those who become believers during the Tribulation be able to participate in the marriage supper of the Lamb?

_____

_____

What will be the effect on relationships between those with perishable bodies and those with immortal bodies in the Millennium?

_____

_____

_____

Why will all nations be expected to observe the Feast of Tabernacles each year during the Millennium?

_____

_____

_____

Who has the responsibility of judging unbelievers and angels?

_____

_____

_____

What does the expression "He will rule them with an iron scepter" (Rev.19:15) mean?

_____

_____

_____

CHAPTER EIGHT

Judgement is Unavoidable

Introduction

There are several events and judgments that take place after the Second Coming of Jesus Christ. They are the judgement of the nations, the First Resurrection, the exercising of judgement by believers, the judgement of Satan and the Great White Throne Judgement.

The interval between the end of Tribulation and the beginning of the Millennium was prophesied by Daniel.

> *"From the time that the daily sacrifice is abolished and the abomination that causes desolation is set up, there will be 1,290 days. Blessed is the one who waits for and reaches the end of the 1,335 days."*
>
> Daniel 12:11-12

The judgement of the nations follows the Second Coming of Jesus Christ but takes place before the believers enter the Millennium; therefore it is the first judgement.

This judgement of the nations concerns how the nations treated the remnant of Jews who refused to worship the Antichrist as god. They were forced to flee the Antichrist in the land of Edom, throughout the second half (1,260 days) of the Great Tribulation, because Satan was determined to kill them and wipe out the whole nation of Israel.

The Judgement of the Nations

All the peoples of the nations will be judged according to how they treated Israel.

> *He will judge between the nations,*
>   *and will settle disputes for many people.*
>
> Isaiah 2:4

131

In the Messianic rule differences will arise between nations which will be resolved by peaceful arbitration from Jerusalem and not by war under Jesus Christ's divine rule.

> *"When the Son of Man comes in his glory, and all the angels with him, he will sit on his glorious throne. All the nations will be gathered before him, and he will separate the people one from another as a shepherd separates the sheep from the goats. He will put the sheep on his right, and the goats on his left. Then the king will say to those on his right, 'Come you who are blessed by my Father; take your inheritance, the kingdom prepared for you since the creation of the world.'"*
>
> *Matthew 25:31-34*

In Israel, shepherds would graze sheep and goats together, but at night they would normally separate the sheep and goats because goats need to be warm at night while the sheep prefer the open air. In ancient texts the right side is for the righteous whereas the left is for the wicked and troublemakers.

> *"For I was hungry and you gave me something to eat, I was thirsty and you gave me something to drink, I was a stranger and you invited me in, I needed clothes and you clothed me, I was sick and you looked after me, I was in prison and you came to visit me."*
>
> *Matthew 25:35-36*

In this prophetic parable, the righteous group ask when they saw him hungry, thirsty, in need of clothing or in prison and responded with kindness.

> *"The King will reply, 'Truly I tell you, whatever you did for one of the least of these brothers and sisters of mine, you did for me.'"*
>
> *Matthew 25:40*

The remainder of the parable relates to the goats who have been separated from the sheep and placed on the left. They were the people that treated the remnant of Jews badly during this intense period of persecution and did not offer them any assistance.

"Then he will say to those on his left, 'Depart from me, you who are cursed, into the eternal fire prepared for the devil and his angels. For I was hungry and you gave me nothing to eat, I was thirsty and you gave me nothing to drink, I was a stranger and you did not take invite me in, I needed clothes and you did not clothe me, I was sick and in prison and you did not look after me.'"

Matthew 25:41-43

The people that did not help the Jews will be condemned to the same punishment that is being prepared for Satan: "the lake of burning sulfur" (Rev.20:10).

This judgement is to be distinguished from the Great White Throne Judgement because there is no resurrection; the persons judged are living nations; no books are opened; the time is at the return of Christ and the scene is on earth.[54]

The First Resurrection

The next event that takes place is termed the First Resurrection.

1. JESUS CHRIST IS THE 'FIRST FRUITS'

The apostle Paul makes it clear to the church at Corinth that Jesus Christ was the first fruits when he defeated death on the cross at Calvary.

But Christ has indeed been raised from the dead, the firstfruits of those who have fallen asleep. For since death came through a man, the resurrection of the dead comes also through a man. For as in Adam all die, so in Christ all will be made alive. But each in turn: Christ, the firstfruits; then, when he comes, those who belong to him. Then the end will come, when he hands over the kingdom to God the Father after he has destroyed all dominion, authority and power. For he must reign until he has put all his enemies under his feet. The last enemy to be destroyed is death.

1 Corinthians 15:20-26

---

[54] See Rev. C. I. Scofield; *The Scofield Reference Bible*

133

2. THE APPEARANCE OF THE HOLY PEOPLE

When Jesus Christ was resurrected from the tomb at Easter, many Old Testament saints were resurrected at the same time. We are told very little about them, other than that they went into Jerusalem and appeared to many people, which must have caused huge interest and surprised them.

> *The bodies of many holy people who had died were raised to life. They came out of the tombs after Jesus' resurrection and went into the holy city and appeared to many people.*
>
> Matthew 27:52-53

> *That these bodies returned to their graves is not said and may not be inferred.*
>
> Rev. C. I. Scofield[55]

These holy people who were raised to life served as witnesses to Jesus Christ's power over death and claim to be the Jewish Messiah.

3. THE DEAD IN CHRIST

The dead in Christ are all those believers who will return to earth at the Rapture of the Church.

> *For the Lord himself will come down from heaven, with a loud command, with the voice of the archangel and with the trumpet call of God, and the dead in Christ will rise first.*
>
> 1 Thessalonians 4:16

> *Brothers and sisters, we do not want you to be uninformed about those who sleep in death, so that you do not grieve like the rest of mankind, who have no hope. For we believe that Jesus died and rose again, and so we believe that God will bring with Jesus those who have fallen asleep in him.*
>
> 1 Thessalonians 4:13-14

---

[55] *The Scofield Reference Bible*

4. THOSE ALIVE AT THE RAPTURE

When the Rapture of living believers occurs, all those who are alive will follow those resurrected believers and will meet with them in the clouds, before they are taken to heaven with Jesus Christ.

> *After that, we who are still alive and are left will be caught up together with them in the clouds to meet the Lord in the air. And so we will be with the Lord forever.*
>
> *1 Thessalonians 4:17*

Those alive when the Rapture takes place will be instantly changed from their earthly perishable bodies into immortal bodies, which will be everlasting.

> *Listen, I tell you a mystery: We will not all sleep, but we will be changed – in a flash, in the twinkling of an eye, at the last trumpet. For the trumpet will sound, the dead will be raised imperishable, and we will be changed. For the perishable must clothe itself with the imperishable, and the mortal with immortality.*
>
> *1 Corinthians 15:51-53*

5. THE TRIBULATION MARTYRS

The Tribulation martyrs are those believers who were beheaded by the Antichrist because they were faithful witnesses to the saving power of Jesus Christ and refused to take the mark of the beast.

> *And I saw the souls of those who had been beheaded because of their testimony about Jesus and because of the word of God. They had not worshipped the beast or its image and had not received its mark on their foreheads or their hands. They came to life and reigned with Christ a thousand years.*
>
> *Revelation 20:4*

These martyrs will be part of the First Resurrection and, like all believers, are referred to as "blessed and holy" (Rev.20:6a).

> *Do not take revenge, my dear friends, but leave room for God's wrath, for it is written: "It is mine to avenge; I will repay," says the Lord.*
>
> *Romans 12:19*

These five groups of believers will be resurrected by Jesus Christ before he sets up his millennial kingdom. They will enter the Millennial Reign of Jesus Christ with immortal bodies.

Judgement by Believers

The first group of believers who have been given authority to judge are the twelve apostles; they will be given overall responsibility for the twelve tribes of Israel. As far as judging by believers is concerned, it does not mean our judging to vindicate or condemn. It means sharing in His authority and rule over certain people; in the disciples' case, it is the twelve tribes of Israel.

> Jesus said to them, "Truly I tell you, at the renewal of all things when the Son of Man sits on his glorious throne, you who have followed me will also sit on twelve thrones, judging the twelve tribes of Israel."
>
> Matthew 19:28

The Greek word *krino* means 'to distinguish, decide and by implication to try'.[56] The apostles will exercise delegated authority from Jesus Christ and have responsibility for the twelve tribes of Israel. They will be expected to guide, arbitrate and make wise decisions. Being given the authority to judge is not the same as making life and death decisions about a person's eternity destiny. The writer of Hebrews makes it clear that God alone has the right to judge and condemn and has promised vengeance on his own people who deny the deity and sacrifice of Jesus Christ on the cross for our sins.

> How much more severely do you think someone deserves to be punished who has trampled the Son of God underfoot, who has treated as an unholy thing the blood of the covenant that sanctified them, and who has insulted the Spirit of grace? For we know him who said, "It is mine to avenge; I will repay," and again, "The Lord will judge his people." It is a dreadful thing to fall into the hands of the living God.
>
> Hebrews 10:29-31

---

[56] *Strong's Exhaustive Concordance of the Bible*

All believers who are part of the First Resurrection are "priests of God and of Christ" (Rev.20:6b) and will also be given authority from Jesus Christ during the Millennial Reign to participate in his reign. "I saw thrones on which were seated those who had been given authority to judge" (Rev.20:4a) means authority to resolve minor disputes but not to condemn.

The apostle Paul makes it clear to the believers at Corinth that they should not take disputes with others to the courts where unbelievers will determine the merits of their case.

He points out that the believers will occupy thrones of judgement when Jesus Christ reigns on earth and they will be expected to help administer the affairs of the nations with wisdom. Paul is rather scathing of them and admits he is trying to make them feel ashamed – "I say this to shame you" (1.Cor.6:5) – because God has great plans and high expectations for his people and they must be able to settle small matters amongst themselves on earth.

> *Do you not know that the Lord's people will judge the world?*
> *And if you are to judge the world, are you not competent to*
> *judge trivial cases?*

1 Corinthians 6:2

The role of believers in relation to the judgement of angels is similar.

> *Do you not know that we will judge angels? How much more*
> *the things of this life!*

1 Corinthians 6:3

In *Dake's Annotated Reference Bible* he suggests:

> *It does not refer to passing sentence on angels, or sending them*
> *to punishment. It does mean that saints will be exalted higher*
> *than angels and will rule them, making decisions for the*
> *administration of the universe.*

John was amazed at what God had revealed to him about the future and, in particular, the new heaven and the new earth. He was so impressed and overcome, he fell down and began to worship at the feet of the angel who had been showing him these things. The angel rebuked him, as this was the second time he had worshipped an angel, and firmly told not to do so, but, "Worship God!" (Rev.19:9b)

"Don't do that! I am a fellow servant with you and with your fellow prophets and with all who keep the words of this scroll."

Revelation 22:9

Most believers do not fully appreciate the importance of our role and place in the kingdom of Jesus Christ. "Now if we are children, then we are heirs – heirs of God and co-heirs with Christ" (Rom.8:17) who will also "reign with him for a thousand years" (Rev.20:6b). Now that is a truly awesome thought!

The Judgement of Satan

At the end of the Millennial Reign of Jesus Christ, Satan has to be released from the Abyss albeit for a short time.

After that he must be set free for a short time.

Revelation 20:3b

It may appear puzzling at first sight why God allows Satan another opportunity to go out and deceive everyone in the world – that is, those born during the Millennium.

During the Millennial Reign, Jesus Christ imposes his perfect and righteous rule on the world and He has not tolerated wickedness and criminal behaviour. People have lived in perfect peace and prospered under a regime where wars and conflict have been eliminated, and calm and tranquillity has been restored. Those born during the Millennium have no experience of life under Satan's power and have not had to choose whom they will serve.

When Satan is let loose Jesus Christ gives those people an opportunity to decide whether they wish to willingly follow and serve Jesus Christ. The alternative is to follow Satan and believe his false promises to satisfy their deepest needs. If they choose Satan, he claims they can indulge every impure thought, selfish desire and ambition.

Sadly, millions will fall for Satan's lies and false promises, and when invited to join his army to overthrow Jesus Christ, will choose to join his great rebellion. Satan will assemble an enormous army from "the four corners of the earth – Gog and Magog" (Rev.20:8) and advance on God's people who are living in the city of Jerusalem. This is Satan's final desperate attempt to destroy the believers and overthrow God. Millions and millions will rebel and join Satan's army. "In number they are like the sand on the seashore" (Rev.20:8b) and they will march across the land and surround Jerusalem. They will have made their choice which confirms mankind has a fallen nature.

...every inclination of the thoughts of the human heart was only evil all the time.

Genesis 6:5b

"The heart is deceitful above all things
*   and beyond cure.*
Who can understand it?"

Jeremiah 17:9

It was a similar story when God rescued the Israelites from slavery at the hands of the Egyptians. In spite of God protecting and providing for their needs in the wilderness, they were unappreciative and unfaithful, which made God angry.

"That is why I was angry with that generation; I said, 'Their hearts are always going astray, and they have not known my ways.'"

Hebrews 3:10

Unlike the Israelites under Moses' leadership, those born during the Millennium have no excuse whatsoever. They have been able to live healthy, satisfying lives in a just and peaceful world under the leadership of Jesus Christ. Despite this, millions are dissatisfied and believe Satan's lies and false promises, and support his attempt to overthrow the kingdom of Jesus Christ and replace Him with Satan. Their actions demonstrate they deserve to live with the consequences of their sinfulness. God is not willing to tolerate any more rebellion; it is time for judgement and punishment.

They marched across the breadth of the earth and surrounded the camp of God's people, the city he loves. But fire came down from heaven and devoured them.

Revelation 20:9

The fire from heaven burns to a cinder this colossal army of Satan. Satan is promptly condemned and receives eternal punishment.

And the devil, who deceived them, was thrown into the fiery lake of burning sulfur, where the beast and the false prophet

139

*had been thrown. They will be tormented day and night for
ever and ever.*

Revelation 20:10

The Great White Throne Judgement

Once Satan and his armies have been completely obliterated in the
fire from heaven, the judgement of unbelievers will follow. This takes
place at the great white throne and Jesus Christ is the judge.

> *"Moreover, the Father judges no one, but has entrusted all
> judgment to the Son, that all may honor the Son just as they
> honor the Father."*

John 5:22-23

All unbelievers will be included in the Second Resurrection that takes
place at the end of the Millennium.

> *(The rest of the dead did not come to life until the thousand
> years were ended.)*

Revelation 20:5

It should be stressed only those who are "dead in [their]
transgressions and sin" (Eph.2:1) because they have rejected Jesus Christ
and declined the offer of salvation, will appear before Him at the great
white throne. Nobody will be able to escape judgement and there will be
nowhere to hide when Jesus Christ comes to judge unbelievers. God is no
respecter of persons and everyone will be included, from the most
wealthy, influential rulers and kings, to the poorest vagabond.

> *Then I saw a great white throne and him who was seated on
> it. The earth and the heavens fled from his presence, and there
> was no place for them. And I saw the dead, great and small,
> standing before the throne, and books were opened.*

Revelation 20:11-12a

Everyone who has ever died since the time of Adam and Eve will be
resurrected, hence the term the Second Resurrection. This will include all
those who died during the Tribulation, all those who were drowned in
the sea, all those who were killed in explosions, or horrendous accidents
or were evaporated as a result of nuclear weapons being deployed. Even
when there are no discernible remains, they will all be resurrected and

appear before Jesus Christ at the great white throne to give an account of their lives to Him.

> *The sea gave up the dead that were in it, and death and Hades gave up the dead that were in them, and each person was judged according to what they had done.*
>
> *Revelation 20:13*

There are three criteria that will be applied to unbelievers at the Great White Throne Judgement when the Book of Life is opened, which will depend on when they were alive on earth.

Judgement by the Law

This aspect of judgement will assess whether a Jewish unbeliever has fully complied with God's law. Given the Gentiles were unaware of God's law they will be judged using another criterion. Failing to keep God's law will condemn the Jews but it is man's heart and conscience that condemns the rest of mankind.

> *For all who rely on the works of the law are under a curse, as it is written: "Cursed is everyone who does not continue to do everything written in the Book of the Law." Clearly no one who relies on the law is justified before God, because the "righteous will live by faith."*
>
> *Galatians 3:10-11*

It is impossible for any human being to fulfil every requirement of the *Torah Mosh,* otherwise known as the Mosaic law, contained in the *Torah* (the first five books of the Hebrew Bible). Paul's letter to the church in Rome makes it clear that God's standard of perfection is not possible for any human to achieve because our basic nature is sinful, corrupt and wicked.

> *The law is not based on faith; on the contrary, it says, "The person who does these things will live by them." Christ redeemed us from the curse of the law by becoming a curse for us, for it is written: "Cursed is everyone who is hung on a pole." He redeemed us in order that the blessing given to Abraham might come to the Gentiles through Christ Jesus, so that by faith we might receive the promise of the Spirit.*
>
> *Galatians 3:12-14*

141

Jesus Christ provided a way for everyone to be saved by dying for the sins of the world on the cross, instead of us. No one is able to meet God's standard of perfection, which is why God sent his son to show us that through faith in Him, we could receive his indwelling Holy Spirit and be made righteous and acceptable to him.

> *"For God did not send his Son into the world to condemn the world, but to save the world through him."*
>
> John 3:17

Everyone is guilty because we have fallen short of his standard of perfection, but God has provided a way for us all to be saved through his underserved grace.

> *There is no difference between Jew and Gentile, for all have sinned and fall short of the glory of God, and all are justified freely by his grace through the redemption that came by Jesus Christ.*
>
> Romans 3:22b-24

It is clear that complying with every detail of the law is not possible for anyone to achieve.

Judgement by Human Works

> *The dead were judged according to what they had done as recorded in the books.*
>
> Revelation 20:12b

Another criterion that will be applied to unbelievers is whether they have lived a pure and righteous life in thought, word and deed. Unbelievers will be judged by what they have done.

The principle of divine judgement is explained by Jesus Christ to Peter in the parable of the unfaithful servant. The servant who knew his master's will but did not do it was punished severely and "beaten with many blows" (Lk.12:47b). In Jewish law "the judge must not impose more than forty lashes" (Deut.25:3a). "But the one who does not know and does things deserving punishment will be beaten with fewer blows." (Lk.12:48a) In Jewish law a petty crime would be punished by four to six lashes. Doing sinful things knowingly will result in heavy condemnation, whereas doing sinful things unknowingly will mean lighter condemnation. Although there are degrees of punishment with God, both result in condemnation.

God keeps a record of everyone's actions, so every hidden thought and action will be exposed when the divine 'filmed recording' of your life is played and every action is examined. This will be supplemented by examining the 'thought recorder' which will expose every secret wish, desire and idea – good and bad – that you ever had. Solomon spoke these prophetic words concerning the final judgement of the wicked:

> *Fear God and keep his commandments,*
> *for this is the duty of all mankind.*
> *For God will bring every deed into judgment,*
> *including every hidden thing,*
> *whether it is good or evil.*

> *Ecclesiastes 12:13-14*

Which prompts one to ask, can anyone cope with that level of scrutiny apart from a divine person, the Lord Jesus Christ? God's verdict on our acts of righteousness is crushing: they are like filthy rags!

> *All of us have become like one who is unclean,*
> *and all our righteous acts are like filthy rags;*
> *we all shrivel up like a leaf,*
> *and like the wind our sins sweep us away.*

> *Isaiah 64:6*

The Book of Life

> *Another book was opened, which is the book of life.*

> *Revelation 20:12*

When the Book of Life is opened, unless your name appears in this book, you will suffer the second death.

> *Anyone whose name was not found written in the book of life*
> *was thrown into the lake of fire.*

> *Revelation 20:15*

This may happen in one of three ways. The first way is to disregard God's warning not to take anything away from this prophecy which is "the revelation from Jesus Christ" (Rev.1:1). Disregarding God's warning is foolish – as is disbelief, which is calling God a liar!

For the wages of sin is death, but the gift of God is eternal life in Christ Jesus our Lord.

Romans 6:23

When people hear the gospel of Jesus Christ but do not believe he is the Son of God and reject him completely, God says they will face judgement and punishment because this prophecy for believers will soon be fulfilled. When a person's heart is far away from God, there are no signs of faith apparent in their lives and their actions demonstrate this fact; Billy Graham describes it as "moral apostasy".

The second way a person's name may not appear in the Book of Life is what Billy Graham describes as "theological apostasy". This can be the result of false teachers who misrepresent the gospel of Jesus Christ and persuade believers to follow their false doctrines. Those who claim to be a Christian but live a wicked and unrighteous life and refuse to repent, may not have genuinely accepted Jesus Christ as Lord of their life.

No one who lives in him keeps on sinning. No one who continues to sin has either seen him or known him.

1 John 3:6

Billy Graham points out that only God knows if a person has truly repented of their sins and given their life to the Lord Jesus Christ.

If we live sinful lives, it may well mean that we haven't given ourselves to Christ after all, and we've even deceived ourselves into thinking we are saved when we really aren't. The Bible warns, 'As the body without the Spirit is dead, so faith without deeds is dead.'[57]

A third way a name may not appear in the Book of Life is if the person has sinned against God by rebelling, becoming apostate and failing to repent. When Moses went up Mount Sinai to receive the Ten Commandments from God, he discovered that during the time he was away the Israelites had made a golden calf which they were worshipping (see Ex.32:4). Moses pleaded with God:

"Please forgive their sin – but if not, then blot me out of the book you have written."

Exodus 32:32

---

[57] *www.billygraham.org.uk:answer-may-29-once;* bible quote from James 2:26

144

However, God was not of a mind to forgive such blatant, sinful behaviour and promised Moses they would be punished.

> *The LORD replied to Moses, "Whoever, has sinned against me I will blot out of my book."*
>
> *Exodus 32:33*

> *Scripture teaches plainly that God blots the names of sinners out of his book.*
>
> *Finis Jennings Dake[58]*

Those Israelites who worshipped the golden calf incurred God's wrath and were punished.

> *And the LORD struck the people with a plague because of what they did with the calf Aaron had made.*
>
> *Exodus 32:35*

However, the Bible promises believers, who are "dressed in white" which is the clothing of righteousness, their names will never be removed from the Book of Life. They will be welcomed into heaven as members of God's family.

> *"The one who is victorious will, like them, be dressed in white. I will never blot out the name of that person from the book of life, but will acknowledge that name before my Father and his angels."*
>
> *Revelation 3:5*

Faithful believers who persevere and are determined to finish the race are those who "Put on the full armor of God, so that you can take your stand against the devil's schemes" (Eph.6:11). A believer whose faith is tested and is victorious, will receive the "crown of life" in heaven.

> *Blessed is the one who perseveres under trial because, having stood the test, that person will receive the crown of life that the Lord has promised to those who love him.*
>
> *James 1:12*

---

[58] *Dake's Annotated Reference Bible*

The Lamb's Book of Life

The apostle John makes it clear that everyone who worships the Antichrist will not be included in the Lamb's Book of Life.

All inhabitants of the earth will worship the beast – all whose names have not been written in the Lamb's book of life, the Lamb who was slain from the creation of the world.

Revelation 13:8

The Lamb's Book of Life contains the names of all those who have accepted Jesus Christ as their personal saviour and have been promised eternal life.

Nothing impure will ever enter it, nor will anyone who does what is shameful or deceitful, but only those whose names are written in the Lamb's book of life.

Revelation 21:27

God is preparing a "new heaven and a new earth" (Rev.21:1) to replace our fallen world for all believers, which will be their eternal future.

They will be his people, and God himself will be with them and be their God.

Revelation 21:3

Points for Reflection

Judgement is something that no unbeliever can avoid. The fate of all those who are unredeemed sinners is made very clear.

But the cowardly, the unbelieving, the vile, the murderers, the sexually immoral, those who practice magic arts, the idolaters and all liars – they will be consigned to the fiery lake of burning sulfur. This is the second death.

Revelation 21:8

A person who accepts Jesus Christ as their saviour and Lord will have their name entered in the Lamb's Book of Life because it is "the Lamb of God, who takes away the sins of the world" (Jn.1:29b). Putting our trust in Jesus Christ is the only way we can be saved and enter into an eternal relationship with our heavenly Father. There is no other way that guarantees avoiding judgement at the great white throne.

God so loved the world that he gave his one and only Son, that whoever believes in him shall not perish but have eternal life.

John 3:16

Questions

What did Jesus mean when he said to the disciples, "...you who have followed me will also sit on twelve thrones, judging the twelve tribes of Israel" (Matt.19:28)?

_____

_____

_____

Do the Tribulation martyrs have a particular role during the Millennial Reign of Jesus Christ?

_____

_____

_____

Is it possible to have your name in the Lamb's Book of Life (see Rev.13:8) but not appear in the Book of Life (see Rev.20:12)?

_____

_____

Is there an opportunity for unbelievers to repent during the Millennial Reign of Jesus Christ?

_____

_____

The Great White Throne Judgement is completely incompatible with the Roman Catholic doctrine of purgatory. Discuss.

_____

_____

_____

Is it possible for anybody to avoid punishment because of their human deeds or their compliance with God's laws?

_____

_____

CHAPTER NINE

A New Heaven and a New Earth

Introduction

God revealed to the prophet Isaiah 2,700 years ago, during the reign of King Hezekiah (716-687 B.C.), "I will create new heavens and a new earth." (Is.65:17a)

We now move forward to A.D. 95 when Jesus Christ confirms in the vision to John that Isaiah's prophecy is accurate and will take place in the future. The new heavens referred to are the atmospheric heaven which surrounds the earth and the stellar heaven which contains the stars and galaxies; but not the third heaven which is where the throne of God is found. It means our atmospheric heaven and our present earth will be destroyed because this is where Satan lives and pollutes our present world.

> *For our struggle is not against flesh and blood, but against the rulers, against the authorities, against the powers of this dark world and against the spiritual forces of evil in the heavenly realms.*
>
> *Ephesians 6:12*

If the Rapture were to occur this week – and be ready because it might – believers will spend seven years in heaven during the time of Tribulation on earth, then return for the Millennial Reign of Jesus Christ. The new creation will follow after judgement has taken place, so we are in a time frame of 1,007 years ahead of now, as a minimum. The earth that we know will be replaced by "a new heaven and a new earth, for the first heaven and the first earth had passed away, and there was no longer any sea" (Rev.21:1). (The Greek word *thalassa* means 'sea'.) The only source of water in the new earth is "the river of the water of life" (Rev.22:1).

The absence of any sea is not explained, but the association with the sea has negative connotations in Scripture. For instance, in the time of

Noah the great flood brought judgement to our wicked world and "the waters flooded the earth for one hundred and fifty days" (Gen.7:24). When the Israelites finally escaped from Egypt and Pharaoh's pursuing army, the "water flowed back and covered the chariots and horsemen – the entire army of Pharaoh that had followed the Israelites into the sea" (Ex.14:28). In this prophecy John witnessed the first beast, the Antichrist, emerging from the sea and being given delegated authority and power from Satan, the dragon, to deceive and rule the world. "The dragon stood on the shore of the sea. And I saw a beast coming out of the sea," (Rev.13:1) and he saw, "The dragon gave the beast his power and great authority." (Rev.13:2b)

The book of Revelation gives us an insight into our distant future which includes the dimensions of our new home in the new holy city of Jerusalem.

> *I saw the Holy City, the new Jerusalem, coming down out of heaven from God, prepared as a bride beautifully dressed for her husband. ... It shone with the glory of God, and its brilliance was like that of a very precious jewel, like a jasper, clear as crystal.*
>
> *Revelation 21:2,11*

The bride of Christ (the Greek word *nymphe* means 'bride'[59]) is the church who will live in this fantastic new city of Jerusalem with God, Jesus Christ and the Holy Spirit .

> *"God's dwelling place is now among the people, and he will dwell with them."*
>
> *Revelation 21:3*

Jesus Christ has declared, "I am making everything new!" (Rev.21:5) and John was told to write everything down, because it is absolutely true, so that God's plans for believers can be appreciated. We will be spending eternity with God in our immortal resurrected bodies:

> *We wait eagerly for our adoption to sonship, the redemption of our bodies.*
>
> *Romans 8:23*

---

[59] *Strong's Exhaustive Concordance of the Bible;* p.1651

The New Jerusalem

One of the angels invited John to, "Come, I will show you the bride, the wife of the Lamb." (Rev.21:9b) The description of the new Jerusalem gives us a glimpse into how perfect our life will be living with Jesus Christ for eternity. (The Greek word *kainos* means 'new'.[60])

> *And he carried me away in the Spirit to a mountain great and high, and showed me the Holy City, Jerusalem, coming down out of heaven from God.*
>
> Revelation 21:10

It is not easy to fully appreciate the significance of all things being "new" in this eternal city, because as humans we cannot understand many things about God, who is transcendent and lives outside our natural world, free of any constraints.

> *Oh, how great are God's riches and wisdom and knowledge! How impossible it is for us to understand his decisions and his ways.*
>
> Romans 11:33 (NLT)

The new city of Jerusalem is almost impossible to visualize due to its awe-inspiring magnificence, because it shines with the glory of God. The main street is paved with gold and looks "as pure as transparent glass" (Rev.21:21b). It is difficult to visualise such an awesome sight as our human minds cannot compare this spectacle with anything known to man. The most highly prized precious stones and minerals, which we consider to be of immense value on earth, are only everyday objects used by God to build roads and construct buildings in the new Jerusalem. On earth we make extensive use of concrete and tarmac for reasons of economy, but God will only provide the very best and most extravagant of materials for his bride's home – the believers.

The Covenant Relationship

John was shown the city surrounded with a very high wall, which was a colossal 144 cubits thick – that is, "216 feet thick" (Rev.21:17, NLT). In each of the four walls there were three gates; each gate was made from a single pearl and on the gates were written the names of the twelve tribes

---

[60] *Strong's Exhaustive Concordance of the Bible;* p.1637

of Israel. Inscribing the names on the gates acts as reminder to celebrate the covenant relationship God made with Israel when he promised them an eternal home.

In the 'Abrahamic Covenant' God promised Israel, "I will make you into a great nation," (Gen.12:2) and in the 'Mosaic Covenant' God promised, "Whenever I cause my name to be honored, I will come to you and bless you." (Exodus 20:24b) In the 'Land of Israel Covenant' God's promise was, "Wherever the LORD your God disperses you among the nations ... Even if you have been banished to the most distant lands under the heavens, from there the LORD your God will gather you and bring you back." (Deut.30:1b,4) The 'New Covenant' was God's promise to Israel that "your children will return to their own land" (Jer.31:17).

> *Remember that at that time you were separate from Christ, excluded from citizenship in Israel and foreigners to the covenants of the promise, without hope and without God in the world. But now in Christ Jesus you who once were far away have been brought near by the blood of Christ.*
>
> *Ephesians 2:12-13*

The twelve tribes of Israel were commanded to observe the law of Moses. This meant the Gentile nations were not included in the blessings that God promised to the Jews. Once Jesus Christ came as the promised Messiah, the barrier that existed between Jews and Gentiles was removed. His death on the cross for the sins of the whole of mankind meant that the gift of salvation and eternal life was available to both Jews and Gentiles.

> *For he himself is our peace, who has made the two groups one and has destroyed the barrier, the dividing wall of hostility, by setting aside in his flesh the law with its commands and regulations. His purpose was to create in himself one new humanity out of the two, thus making peace, and in one body to reconcile both of them to God through the cross, by which he put to death their hostility.*
>
> *Ephesians 2:14-16*

The twelve foundations are inscribed with the names of the twelve apostles to ensure we always remember the twelve disciples of Jesus Christ who were given the Great Commission to bring the good news of salvation to the whole world. This was the means for everyone to be saved from eternal punishment for their sins and to be saved by the grace of God. We can all be members of God's family which is "built on the foundation of the apostles and prophets, with Christ Jesus as the chief cornerstone" (Eph.2:20).

These enormous, impregnable walls and gates are not there for defensive purposes, because nothing impure and unholy will be permitted to enter the city. The gates in ancient cities like Jerusalem would be closed at night for security reasons, but the gates in the new Jerusalem will never be shut because there will be no intruders, only kings and leaders of different countries wanting to enter Jerusalem to honour and worship God.

> It had a great, high wall, with twelve gates, and with twelve angels at the gates. On the gates were written the names of the twelve tribes of Israel. There were three gates on the east, three on the north, three on the south and three on the west. The wall of the city had twelve foundations, and on them were the names of the twelve apostles of the Lamb.
>
> Revelation 21:12-14

The purpose of these walls and gates is simply to glorify God with their unsurpassed beauty, strength and magnificence.

The Dimensions of the City

When the angel measured the city with his gold measuring rod, the length, width and height of the city were identical and came to 12,000 stadia (1,500 miles) which is the shape of a cube. The size of the new city of Jerusalem is comparable to the United States of America but extends 1,500 miles into the sky.

> The angel who talked with me had a measuring rod of gold to measure the city, its gates and its walls. The city was laid out like a square, as long as it was wide. He measured the city with the rod and found it to be 12,000 stadia in length, and as wide and high as it is long. The angel measured the wall using human measurement, and it was 144 cubits thick.
>
> Revelation 21:15-17

How this vast height will be utilised is difficult to envisage and some scholars think it may be layered. If this is the case, it has been suggested a penthouse in a skyscraper 1,500 miles high would have incredible but indescribable views. Much of what is implied is hard to imagine because the earth's atmosphere only extends to fifty miles above the surface of the earth. Such a splendid creation can only be understood if you believe the laws of physics will not have any relevance in God's new creation.

There are many references to the number twelve or multiples of twelve in this new city, which is a holy number associated with the government and administration of the new heavens and earth. The size of the city is twelve thousand stadia; there are twelve gates with twelve angels at the gates; on the gates are the names of the twelve tribes of Israel. The names of the twelve apostles are written on the twelve layers of foundations supporting the city walls (see Rev.21:12-14).

The Foundations

The foundations of the city walls produce a spectacular display of dazzling colour. They contain every kind of anisotropic stone, which reflect all the colours in the spectrum, irrespective of their original colour.

> *The foundations of the city walls were decorated with every kind of precious stone. The first foundation was jasper, the second sapphire, the third agate, the fourth emerald, the fifth onyx, the sixth ruby, the seventh chrysolite, the eighth beryl, the ninth topaz, the tenth turquoise, the eleventh jacinth, and the twelfth amethyst.*

Revelation 21:19-20

The qualities of each stone mentioned in the foundations are as follows:

1. <u>Jasper</u> is a smooth opaque variety of chalcedony usually brown, yellow or a reddish colour.
2. <u>Sapphire</u> is a blue precious gemstone which comes in a variety of colours, including violet, green, yellow, orange, pink and purple. Some stones manifest the phenomenon known as colour change, going from blue in daylight to purple under incandescent lighting.
3. <u>Agate</u> occurs in a wide range of colours, including brown, white, red, grey, pink, black and yellow. It is a finely grained microcrystalline quartz mineral rock.

4. <u>Emerald</u> is a green beryl stone that emits the purest green ray energy.
5. <u>Onyx</u> is a black cryptocrystalline, consisting of fine intergrowths of quartz and moganite, formed by bands of chalcedony in alternating colours.
6. <u>Ruby</u> is a pink to blood-red gemstone.
7. <u>Chrysolite</u> is gold mixed with green and comes with a fine lustre.
8. <u>Beryl</u> is a sea-green stone composed of beryllium aluminium cyclosilicate and occurs in a variety of colours, but the green variety is called emerald.
9. <u>Topaz</u> is a precious rich wine-yellow stone with occasional pale tinges of green or red.
10. <u>Turquoise</u> is an opaque blue-to-green gemstone with a unique hue and has been highly prized for thousands of years as a gemstone and ornamental stone. This gemstone was originally mined in Persia and first brought to Europe through Turkey.
11. <u>Jacinth</u> is an orange-red transparent variety of zircon used as a gemstone.
12. <u>Amethyst</u> is a violet-blue variety of quartz.

The Absent Temple

John was struck by the absence of a temple in the city.

I did not see a temple in the city because the Lord God Almighty and the Lamb are its temple.

Revelation 21:22

In the eternal kingdom that follows the Millennium it will become evident that a temple is not necessary as sin will be absent and the only people admitted to the heavenly new Jerusalem will be believers.

God's original plan was that Adam would supervise every living thing in his wonderful creation and he desired a close relationship with him. When Adam and Eve disobeyed his commandment, this allowed sin to enter the world and defile God's creation.

"Cursed is the ground because of you."

Genesis 3:17b

God had to remove them both from the Garden of Eden and make it impossible for them to regain entry, otherwise Adam and Eve could have access to the tree of life and sinful humans would have become immortal.

> *"He must not be allowed to reach out his hand and take also from the tree of life and eat, and live forever."*
>
> *Genesis 3:22b*

The outcome was physical death in line with God's curse on mankind:

> *"By the sweat of your brow you will eat your food until you return to the ground, since from it you were taken; for dust you are and to dust you will return."*
>
> *Genesis 3:19*

God's love for us is intense and although we have misused his gift of free will, he has persevered with His relationship with us.

> *"Then have them make a sanctuary for me, and I will dwell among them. Make this tabernacle and all its furnishings exactly like the pattern I will show you."*
>
> *Exodus 25:8-9*

In the millennial kingdom there will be a temple for people to worship God because those born during the Millennium must have the opportunity to choose whether or not to worship God.

There will be no need for a temple in the eternal order, as God himself will be living there with his Son and with the Holy Spirit. This will make not only the Holy City one grand and glorious temple or place of worship, but also the eternal earth.[61]

The Glory of God

The holy city of Jerusalem is the bride and Jesus Christ is the bridegroom. Only those who have been born again and redeemed by the blood of the Lamb will be able to gain access.

> *The nations will walk by its light, and the kings of the earth will bring their splendor into it. On no day will its gates ever*

---

[61] See Tim LaHaye; *Revelation Unveiled;* p.364

be shut, for there will be no night there. The glory and honor of the nations will be brought into it.

Revelation 21:24-26

During the reign of King Hezekiah, Isaiah prophesied:

"The sun will no more be your light by day,
  nor will the brightness of the moon shine on you,
for the LORD will be your everlasting light,
  and your God will be your glory."

Isaiah 60:19

Jesus also said he was "the bright Morning Star" (Rev.22:16). Although the city will not need the sun and moon to shine, it does not mean they will cease to exist. Instead, the brilliance of the glory of the godhead will provide sufficient lighting to ensure "there will be no night there" (Rev.21:25b).

The city does not need the sun or the moon to shine on it, for the glory of God gives it light, and the Lamb is its lamp.

Revelation 21:23

An angel takes John on a tour of the city and sees "the river of the water of life" which flows as clear as crystal from God's throne down the middle of the street of gold. On either side of the river stands the "tree of life" which astonishingly produces twelve crops of ripe fruit every month (see Rev.22:1-2).

However, the most amazing revelation is that God has chosen to make his home in the new Jerusalem with us, his family of believers.

"God's dwelling place is now among the people, and he will dwell with them."

Revelation 21:3a

Our Guaranteed Future

The concept of living for eternity is quite difficult to grasp, even though many unbelievers foolishly live their lives as if there is no tomorrow and they will live forever.

There will be no more sadness, pain or death because our immortal bodies will enjoy perfect health and everlasting happiness, as was prophesied by Isaiah:

> *"...the sound of weeping and of crying*
> *will be heard in it no more."*
>
> Isaiah 65:19b

Memories of our former lives that might trouble us in the future will cease to have any hold over us.

> *"The former things will not be remembered,*
> *nor will they come to mind."*
>
> Isaiah 65:17b

> *"'He will wipe away every tear from their eyes. There will be no more death' or mourning or crying or pain, for the old order of things has passed away."*
>
> Revelation 21:4

In God's new eternal creation his original plan will be achieved because sin will have been eradicated and the earth will no longer suffer the curse of Satan. No one will ever feel alone or marginalised or undervalued in this new eternal creation because we will all be able to enjoy fellowship with one another as we worship God.

> *Then I looked and heard the voice of many angels, numbering thousands upon thousands, and ten thousand times ten thousand ... In a loud voice they were saying:*
> *"Worthy is the Lamb, who was slain,*
> *to receive power and wealth and wisdom and strength*
> *and honor and glory and praise."*
>
> Revelation 5:11a-12

A Perfect Life

We are only given a taste of what our lives will be like in this new creation, but we know that our new home is designed for sinless, perfected believers who have been sealed and belong to God.

> *The throne of God and of the Lamb will be in the city, and his servants will serve him. They will see his face, and his name will be on their foreheads.*
>
> Revelation 22:3-4

We will have a life free from the stress, pressure and worry we have experienced in a fallen world. It will be a time of praise, worship and enjoyment in the presence of God as his children.

"Yes," says the Spirit, "they will rest from their labor, for their deeds will follow them."

Revelation 14:13b

We will live holy, pure, sanctified lives, because nothing unrighteous will ever be allowed to enter the holy City.

The glory and honor of the nations will be brought into it. Nothing impure will enter it, nor will anyone who does what is shameful or deceitful, but only those whose names are written in the Lamb's book of life.

Revelation 21:26-27

Our life of joy and happiness will be enhanced by being able to serve God.

The throne of God and of the Lamb will be in the city, and his servants will serve him.

Revelation 22:3

"To the thirsty I will give water without cost from the spring of the water of life. Those who are victorious will inherit all this, and I will be their God and they will be my children."

Revelation 21:6-7

We will enjoy the most glorious praise and worship and have fellowship with millions of like-minded people, including family, relatives and friends who share the same desire to wholeheartedly serve God.

After this I heard what sounded like the roar of a great multitude in heaven shouting:
"Hallelujah!
Salvation and glory and power belong to our God,
for true and just are his judgments."

Revelation 19:1-2a

Points for Reflection

When Daniel had his second vision, during the reign of Belshazzar, it was a prophecy about other nations who would overcome and follow on after the fall of the Babylonian empire. They were represented by the "ram" and the "goat". The two-horned ram represented the kings of Medes and Persia and the shaggy goat concerned the king of Greece (see Dan.8:20-21).

> *"The vision of the evenings and mornings that has been given to you is true, but seal up the vision, for it concerns the distant future."*
>
> Daniel 8:26

This time, the apostle John is told by the angel not to seal up this prophecy, because it concerns events that will soon be taking place.

> *"Do not seal up the words of the prophecy of this scroll, because the time is near."*
>
> Revelation 22:10

The time is fast approaching when Jesus Christ is returning for his church. This fact is emphasised twice in the final verses of this prophecy to "his servants". He is speaking directly to believers to give us hope, assurance and peace about our glorious future, which begins once Jesus Christ comes back to rapture the church.

> *"These words are trustworthy and true. The Lord, the God who inspires the prophets, sent his angel to show his servants the things that must soon take place."*
>
> Revelation 22:6 (NIV)

While we wait for these events to occur, there is a final word of encouragement to the church. We are the bride of Jesus Christ and must ensure, like the Galilean brides, to keep ourselves faithful, pure and holy while we wait for our bridegroom the Lord Jesus Christ to come.

> *"Let the one who does right continue to do right; and let the holy person continue to be holy."*
>
> Revelation 22:11b

Questions

This prophecy contains a serious warning about adulterating the word of God (see Rev.22:18-19). Does that warning apply to all scripture in the Bible?

_____

_____

What is the significance of "the free gift of water of life" (Rev.22:17)?

_____

_____

Who is the "Alpha and Omega" (Rev.22:13) and what does it mean?

_____

_____

Why did John keep worshipping an angel (see Rev.22:8)?

_____

_____

Why is there "no longer any sea" (Rev.21:1) in the new earth and new heaven?

_____

_____

What aspect of the Galilean wedding does the new Jerusalem represent (see Rev.21:9-10)?

_____

_____

_____

Interlude

At this point in the revealing of the prophecy of Jesus Christ, we come to the chronological end of the book of Revelation. However, we will now return to the first three chapters to consider the special message Jesus Christ has for his bride the church. It is a disappointing message for many churches because the bridegroom wants his bride to be holy and spotless and this is not always the case. The message is a challenging, prophetic, contemporary one for the church which we will examine together with the action proposed by Jesus Christ. The book of Revelation closes with this assurance: "Surely, I come quickly." (Rev.20:20, KJV) The Rapture of the Church will be sudden and soon. This poem by Alec Prowse reminds us we are waiting expectantly for this to take place:

The Rapture[62]

When our Lord Jesus ascended back to heaven,
  two angels made this prophetic claim,
That after God's appointed time,
  this same Jesus would return again.
One day he will return and rule the world,
  but before we shall witness many things,
For God's word tells us of perilous times
  before he reigns as king of kings.

But when he returns the first time
  it will be into the air,
And all his blood-bought children
  will be caught up to meet him there.
The event will end God's days of grace,
  there will be no chance tomorrow
For those who have rejected his mercy,
  it will mean only loss, fear and sorrow.

---

[62] Reproduced by kind permission of Alec Prowse

The truth is not preached as it once was,
 but Jesus made it quite plain
To his disciples before he went saying,
 "If I go, I will come again."
If now I have gained your interest
 and you feel you would like to know more,
Turn to Paul's first Thessalonian epistle
 and read what it says in chapter four.

There it is all recorded,
 the order of events so profound,
Our Lord will appear with a shout and trumpet call,
 and the dead will be raised from the ground.
At the same time, all God's redeemed people
 will be caught up to meet him in the air,
And we will be together forever,
 for there will be no more partings up there.

Our God will bring all this to fruition
 quicker than we can fly,
In fact, his holy word declares in a moment,
 in the twinkling of an eye,
What a tremendous prospect,
 how long will our saviour delay?
Are you waiting in anticipation?
 For he could return today.

Brothers and sisters, we do not want you to be uninformed about those who sleep in death, so that you do not grieve like the rest of mankind, who have no hope. For we believe that Jesus died and rose again, and so we believe that God will bring with Jesus those who have fallen asleep in him. According to the Lord's word, we tell you that we who are still alive, who are left until the coming of the Lord, will certainly not precede those who have fallen asleep. For the Lord himself will come down from heaven, with a loud command, with the voice of the archangel and with the trumpet call of God, and the dead in Christ will rise first. After that, we who are still alive and are left will be caught up together with them in the clouds to meet the Lord in the air. And so we will be with the Lord forever. Therefore encourage one another with these words.

1 Thessalonians 4:13-18

CHAPTER TEN

A Prophetic Message to the Churches

Introduction

One of the things that is unique about this book is it promises a special blessing to everyone who reads it.

> *Blessed is the one who reads aloud the words of this prophecy,*
> *and blessed are those who hear it and take to heart what is*
> *written in it, because the time is near.*
>
> *Revelation 1:3*

The timeline for the events in Revelation can often cause misunderstanding because God does not view time the same way we use time to regulate our lives. David the songwriter and composer wrote:

> *A thousand years in your sight*
> *are like a day that has just gone by,*
> *or like a watch in the night.*
>
> *Psalm 90:4*

When the apostle Peter was imprisoned in Rome by emperor Nero in A.D. 65 he said:

> *But do not forget this one thing, dear friends: With the Lord a*
> *day is like a thousand years, and a thousand years are like a*
> *day.*
>
> *2 Peter 3:8*

Peter also reminds us that Jesus always keeps his promises and is patient with our sinful world, because he does not want anybody to suffer eternal punishment.

The Lord is not slow in keeping his promise, as some understand slowness. Instead he is patient with you, not wanting anyone to perish, but everyone to come to repentance.

2 Peter 3:9

Many historians date this revelation to John around A.D. 95, at the end of the reign of Roman Emperor Domitian, about forty years after Jesus' physical ascension from this earth to the presence of God in heaven. The vision occurred during the time when John was imprisoned in a Roman penal colony on the Island of Patmos (8 miles x 4 miles), one of several islands named the Dodecanese, located south-east of the Aegean Sea.

"Write on a scroll what you see and send it to the seven churches: to Ephesus, Smyrna, Pergamum, Thyatira, Sardis, Philadelphia and Laodicea."

Revelation 1:11

John's communication to the seven churches took the form of a pastoral letter and contained a special message to the angel of each church from Jesus Christ. In his role as head of the church, Jesus has the wisdom and insight to discern the churches' true spiritual state. He wanted each church to be aware of his overall assessment of their spiritual health so they could learn from each other. This is the reason John's letter was addressed "to the seven churches in the province of Asia" (Rev.1:4). The province of Asia was in the Roman administrative divisions of the Roman Empire which is modern day Turkey.

Lampstands and Stars

John describes seeing seven golden lampstands and Jesus in all his heavenly glory as he walked amongst the lampstands, with seven stars in his right hand and a sharp double-edged sword in his mouth. The imagery used in this prophecy is explained:

"The seven stars are the angels (divine messengers) of the seven churches, and the seven lampstands are the seven churches."

Revelation 1:20 (AMP)

Moses reminds us of the magnificence of the lampstands God designed to stand in the holy place in the Tabernacle. Each lampstand

167

was made from a *kikkar* which was a talent of pure gold weighing about 75 lbs. It was so valuable, it meant the average labourer would have to work for twenty years to pay for a single lampstand. Each lampstand supported seven lamps and comprised six branches, three branches on each side. Each branch contained three cups shaped like almond flowers with buds and blossoms attached.

> *"Then make its seven lamps and set them up on it so that they light the space in front of it."*
>
> Exodus 25:37

These golden lampstands provided light to the tabernacle, in the same way Jesus is our spiritual light and the church reflects his light to the world.

The seven stars represent the guardian angels Jesus has appointed to protect the churches and act as his messengers to the church. Jesus continually appraises the spiritual faithfulness of all churches to see how well they are obeying his teaching to nourish the body of the church with sound teaching and carry out his Great Commission to faithfully preach the gospel in order to win souls for his Kingdom.

> *So Christ himself gave the apostles, the prophets, the evangelists, the pastors and teachers, to equip his people for works of service, so that the body of Christ may be built up until we all reach unity in the faith and in the knowledge of the Son of God and become mature, attaining to the whole measure of the fullness of Christ.*
>
> Ephesians 4:11-13

When John meets the resurrected Jesus, he is clothed in all his radiant glory, dressed from head to feet in a long robe with a golden sash around his chest. His hair was completely white, his eyes resembled a blazing fire and his feet shone like bronze glows in a furnace. His magnificence and radiance so overwhelmed John that he was completely overcome and fell prostrate at his feet in worship (see Rev.1:17). When he spoke his voice sounded like rushing water.

> *"I am the Alpha and Omega,"* says the Lord God, *"who is, and who was, and who is to come, the Almighty."*
>
> Revelation 1:8

This is a complete contrast to Isaiah's prophetic description of Jesus when he ministers on earth as an ordinary human being.

> *He had no beauty or majesty to attract us to him,*
>   *nothing in his appearance that we should desire him.*
> *He was despised and rejected by mankind,*
>   *a man of suffering and familiar with pain.*

Isaiah 53:2b-3

However, one day all believers will see Jesus Christ in all his regal splendour. On his robe and on his thigh he will have this name written: "KING OF KINGS AND LORD OF LORDS" (Rev.19:16).

Four Interpretations

In the *Scofield Reference Bible,* the Rev. C. I. Scofield (1943-1921) identifies four ways these letters to the seven churches can be interpreted. At its simplest level, the letter contains a local assessment of the spiritual state of each of the seven churches at that time.

The second level concerns advice and warnings that apply to all churches throughout the ages, to the present day, so they can apply these tests to themselves and discern their true spiritual state in the sight of God.

The third level encourages the individual believer to examine their own spiritual state and invites them to learn the lessons and apply them to themselves:

> *"To the one who is victorious, I will give the right to sit with me on my throne, just as I was victorious and sat down with my Father on his throne. Whoever has ears, let them hear what the Spirit says to the churches."*

Revelation 3:21-22

The fourth level is prophetic and covers seven phases in the spiritual history of the church from the time of Pentecost until the end of time. This view of church history is known as the 'historical – prophetic' view as the *Scofield Reference Bible* explains:

> *These messages must cover that fore view if it is in the book at all, for the church does not appear after Revelation 3 : 22.*

Most conclusively of all, these messages do present an exact fore view.

Rev. C. I. Scofield[63]

The Seven Stages of Church History

There is general agreement amongst scholars that the seven churches represent seven sequential stages of church history, although there is not universal agreement about the dates. Whilst all seven types of these churches will always exist at any given period of time, a particular era in church history tends to be represented by one particular church.

EPHESUS REPRESENTS THE APOSTOLIC CHURCH (A.D. 30-100)

The Apostolic Church age commences with the Great Commission when Jesus commissioned his disciples to preach the gospel throughout the world.

> *Then Jesus came to them and said, "All authority in heaven and on earth has been given to me. Therefore go and make disciples of all nations, baptizing them in the name of the Father and of the Son and of the Holy Spirit, and teaching them to obey everything I have commanded you. And surely I am with you always, to the very end of the age."*
>
>

Matthew 28:18-20

A significant date was the "day of Pentecost" (Acts.2:1), when the Holy Spirit descended on believers empowering them to witness about Jesus Christ and enabling them to exercise spiritual gifts under the power of the Holy Spirit.

> *All of them were filled with the Holy Spirit and began to speak in other tongues as the Spirit enabled them.*
>
>

Acts 2:4

This was a time of intense evangelism and vigorous church growth, under dynamic leaders who believed the return of Jesus Christ might occur during their lifetime.

This period covers the Jewish revolt which led to the siege and subsequent destruction of Jerusalem and its temple, under Roman

---

[63] *The Scofield Reference Bible*

General Titus in A.D. 70, which Jesus prophesied at the Mount of Olives: "When you see Jerusalem being surrounded by armies, you will know that its desolation is near." (Lk.21:20) Jesus Christ also told his disciples, "Truly I tell you, not one stone here will be left on another; every one will be thrown down." (Matt.24:2)

According to Josephus, a first century historian, the number who died in the resultant violence and famine was approximately one million people. This led to the Diaspora, which in Greek means 'to scatter about'. The was the start of the second exile of the Jews who were scattered throughout the whole world. This exile lasted for the next 1900 years, until Israel was restored to their own land on 14 May 1948.

SMYRNA REPRESENTS THE PERSECUTED CHURCH (A.D. 100-313)

This period, termed the Persecuted Church, was one when intense persecution of Christians took place at the hands of Roman Emperors Nero, Decius and Diocletian. This unparalleled persecution culminated in Diocletian making it a criminal offence to be a Christian in A.D. 303. However, this persecution only served to strengthen Christianity, and Satan's attacks on the church have since been more subtle and deceptive in this country.

This church period was characterised by cruel persecution by the Romans who brought Christians into the amphitheatre in Rome. There, thousands of spectators would be entertained by the spectacle of Christians being fed to hungry lions. Other believers were crucified, tortured to death by wild animals, burned at the stake, or covered in tar and set on fire to act as human torches.

During this period hundreds of thousands of Christians were martyred by the Romans but Emperor Diocletian's persecution proved to be counterproductive because the church thrived, grew stronger and increased in numbers. Those brave believers in the persecuted church who defended the faith against false teaching and false messiahs, inspired others with their heroic example.

PERGAMUM REPRESENTS THE STATE CHURCH (CIRCA A.D. 313-590)

Emperor Constantine succeeded Diocletian and, after he received a vision from God in the form of a cross in the sky, declared Christianity an official state religion. He permitted Christianity to flourish, and provided protection, finance and even allowed Christians to take over the running of many pagan temples. However, state patronage led the church to make theological compromises in their desire to please the emperor and rulers that followed. This had the effect of allowing unbiblical theology to creep in.

The Roman Catholic Church traces its history back to Jesus Christ and the apostles. It developed its philosophy and doctrines which were different from the Christian church in the second and third centuries. The doctrines and practices that differed from the established church included the following:

A.D. 300 Prayers for the dead.
A.D. 375 The worship of saints and angels.
A.D. 394 The celebration of Mass.
A.D. 431 The worship of Mary.
A.D. 500 Priests began wearing different clothing to lay people.
A.D. 600 Worship services were conducted in Latin.
A.D. 600 Prayers were offered to Mary.

The church of Pergamum, which means 'married', became inextricably wedded to the government of Rome. Although state patronage gave the church political credibility, wealth and influence resulted in its spiritual decline, and its evangelical ministry lacked power and became ineffective.

During A.D. 367-404 all scholars agreed that all of the 27 New Testament books were divinely inspired and Saint Jerome (A.D. 347-420) translated the Bible into Latin, a translation that became known as the Vulgate.

The doctrine of imminency, which had accompanied a surge in evangelical activity, gradually began to be replaced by postmillennialism, leading to the adoption of a more indifferent approach to teaching about the Rapture.

THYATIRA REPRESENTS THE PAPAL CHURCH (CIRCA A.D. 590-1517)

The Papal Church is also known as the 'church of the dark ages'. Monasteries were built and unbiblical teaching became firmly established in the Roman Catholic Church, as the following shows:

A.D. 607 Boniface became the first pope.

A.D. 787 The Nicaean Council approved the use of sacred images to enhance worship.

A.D. 850 Holy water was introduced and, after being blessed by a member of the clergy, was used in baptisms and to bless individuals and articles of devotion.

A.D. 995 The canonisation of dead saints took place.

A.D. 1079 The celibacy of the priesthood was introduced.

A.D. 1190 The sale of Indulgences (in Latin, *indulgentia*) commenced. This was used as a way of reducing the severity and amount of punishment required to atone for sins and a reminder of the importance of penance, which is the confession of sins to a priest to obtain ecclesiastical forgiveness. The church stopped the sale of indulgences in 1567, but Pope John Paul authorized their reintroduction by bishops in 2000 as part of the church's third millennium celebrations.

A.D. 1215 The doctrine of transubstantiation was introduced, which is the belief the eucharistic elements are literally changed into the body and blood of Jesus Christ, with only the appearance of the bread and wine remaining.

A.D. 1220 The Adoration of the Wafer refers to the sacred status of the sacramental bread.

A.D. 1229 It was forbidden for lay persons to have their own copy of the Bible until 1958 when Pope John XXIII encouraged Catholic worshippers to read the 'Confraternity Bible', an English translation of the Catholic Bible which led to many Catholics becoming Christians.

A.D. 1439 The doctrine of Purgatory was introduced which is the belief that the purification of the soul can take place in preparation for admittance to heaven.

A.D. 1545 The status of the Roman Catholic tradition was granted equal standing with the Bible.

A.D. 1546 The apocryphal books were included in the Bible, even though not part of the 'canon of scripture'.

A.D. 1854 The immaculate conception of Mary.

A.D. 1870 The infallibility of the Pope.

A.D. 1965 Mary was proclaimed the Mother of the Church.

In A.D. 610 Islam was founded and Muhammad declared himself the 'Prophet of Allah' and wrote the *Quran* (Koran). Following a bitter dispute about Mohammad's successor in A.D. 632, two main rival sects were formed: the Sunnis and Shias.

Between A.D. 650-1250 Muslim armies invaded Persia, known as Iran since 1935, and conquered the Middle East and North Africa, where an Islamic Caliphate covering five million square miles was established.

SARDIS REPRESENTS THE CHURCH OF THE REFORMATION (CIRCA. A.D. 1517-1790)

The Protestant reformation developed as a reaction to the continued emphasis by the church of Rome on unbiblical doctrine in preference to the inspired, infallible teaching contained in the Bible. Martin Luther encouraged a resurgence of studying the scriptures and published ninety-five theses criticising Roman church practices. As a consequence, in 1521 he was forced to appear before the 'Diet of Worms' where he was excommunicated and declared an "obstinate heretic".

The church in Sardis gained the reputation of being dead and ineffective because it became the state church. A willingness to be subject to regulations and a desire to please the governing authorities meant the emphasis on a personal relationship with Jesus Christ was sublimated to the needs of the whole population. Martin Luther sought the approval of political leaders for the Lutheran church to become the state church in Germany, as did others throughout Europe. This meant infant baptism and sprinkling, formal worship, the emphasis on rituals and the doctrine of transubstantiation continued, which had a deadening effect on the work of the Holy Spirit.

Despite the good intentions of the Puritans who aimed to cleanse the church from all Roman ideas (1580-1800) and revivals initiated by John Wesley and Moody (1730-1800), the reformation period had little lasting effect on the customs and teaching propagated by the Church of Rome. Although it started well, sadly it failed in its endeavours to reform the church and eliminate unbiblical pagan practices.

PHILADELPHIA REPRESENTS THE MISSIONARY CHURCH (CIRCA A.D. 1790-1900)

This church at Philadelphia represents the age of the great missionary movement. Large number of missionary societies were formed with a burning desire to evangelise the world. This led to thousands of missionaries going out to Africa, Nigeria, Burma, China, Japan, Korea, India, South America and many other countries. Two notable preachers, William Carey and Hudson Taylor, renewed bold and energetic preaching of the gospel of Jesus Christ, which led to a revival taking place across Europe, the United Kingdom and America.

The ability to print the Bible in many different languages gave the missionary movement a huge impetus and a resurged interest in studying the doctrine of the Second Coming of Jesus Christ. Renewed interest in the doctrine of the premillennial return of Jesus Christ was ignited around 1800, which had lain dormant since the third century. All these factors contributed to a fresh and zealous interest in evangelism and missionary work. During this period the church was determined to fulfil the 'Great Commission' and prepare for Jesus Christ's return to rapture the church.

During the period A.D. 1780-1900, Christians became active in addressing many social ills, including slavery, alcohol abuse, women's rights and child labour in the United Kingdom, Africa and America. Some key figures of the era were:

- William Wilberforce (1779-1833) who led the movement to abolish the slave trade;
- Frances Willard (1839-1898) who formed the Christian Temperance Movement;
- George Mueller (1805-1898) who built children's homes for orphans;
- Robert Raikes (1735-1811) who founded the Sunday School movement and provided education for 1.25 million children, prior to the English state schooling system that was introduced in 1880.

LAODICEA REPRESENTS THE APOSTATE CHURCH (A.D. 1900 - PRESENT DAY)

The Apostate Church age represents the church at Laodicea and is an indictment of this period of church history. There is little to commend the churches during this period.

Billy Graham considered Jesus Christ's examination of the seven churches in Asia as "an indictment on the church today". It is sadly true that when a church turns away from God's word and pursues worldly values they will inevitably stumble and fall. Tim LaHaye sums up the state of the modern Laodicean church as "the apostate ecumenical church that is gathering momentum".

> *There is a crisis today of many professing Christians walking hand in hand with the world making it difficult to distinguish the Christian from the unbeliever. This should never be. The church was designed to proclaim God's love and forgiveness to all people and declare that Jesus came to eradicate sin in people's hearts. Pastors today would do well to take up a serious study of these letters to the seven churches with their congregations.*
>
> Billy Graham [64]

Many positive ministries started earlier in the 20th century:

- William Booth (1829-1920) originally formed the Christian Mission, which he renamed the Salvation Army in 1878.
- Billy Graham (1918-2018), one of the most influential Christian leaders in the 20th century, preached to 215 million people in 185 countries in the period 1940-1960.
- Louis Palau (b. 1934 – now 86 years old), a retired international evangelist since 1960, said of his ministry, "God is not dis-illusioned with us. He never had any illusions to begin with!"

The apostle Paul said, "But mark this: There will be terrible times in the last days," (2.Tim.3:1) and proceeded to describe in great clarity our contemporary society.

> *People will be lovers of themselves, lovers of money, boastful, proud, abusive, disobedient to their parents, ungrateful, unholy, without love, unforgiving, slanderous, without self-control, brutal, not lovers of the good, treacherous, rash, conceited, lovers of pleasure rather than lovers of God – having a form of godliness but denying its power. Have nothing to do with such people.*
>
> 2 Timothy 3:2-5

---

[64] *https://billygraham.org/answers;* January 23, 2020

The 21st Century Church

We currently enjoy wonderful opportunities to rapidly respond to natural disasters and provide humanitarian aid within hours to any part of the world. Never has a society had so many varied and incredible opportunities to share the gospel thanks to modern travel, the medium of broadcasting and tremendous technological and communication advances.

The book of Revelation provides a prophetic insight into the state of the 21st century church. Many churches neglect to be active, evangelical or teach the imminency of the Rapture and the importance of being ready for the Lord's return. The 21st century church has become complacent and ignorant about this important teaching. Jesus wanted his church and all believers to understand this prophecy as it provides hope, encouragement and reassurance to believers that their glorious future is assured.

It should be apparent to those who read Revelation that no letters to the church appear after the end of Revelation 3. The following chapters, 4-18, are concerned with events during the time of Tribulation. The church of believers is not mentioned during this period of great suffering because all believers will already have been raptured, as they were promised they would be spared the outpouring of the "wrath" of God.

> *They tell how you turned to God from idols to serve the living and true God, and to wait for his Son from heaven, whom he raised from the dead – Jesus, who rescues us from the coming wrath.*

> *1 Thessalonians 1:9-10*

The church of born again believers reappears in chapter 19 and they are now in heaven expressing great joy.

> *"For the wedding of the Lamb has come,*
> *and his bride has made herself ready."*

> *Revelation 19:7b*

This occurs shortly before Jesus returns to earth in the Second Coming.

The 'wedding of the Lamb' refers to the marriage between Jesus Christ and the church which has already taken place in heaven and includes "all the saints of all ages from Abel to the last one of the first resurrection – those who will go to live in the New Jerusalem"[65].

> *Then an angel said to me, "Write this: Blessed are those who are invited to the wedding supper of the Lamb."*
>
> *Revelation 19:9*

Prior to the wedding feast in heaven, all believers will have been raptured and the manner of their departure will leave the world bewildered, confused and in great anguish. (The Greek word *harpazo* means to be 'snatched away'.)

> *Listen, I tell you a mystery: We will not all sleep, but we will all be changed – in a flash, in the twinkling of an eye, at the last trumpet. For the trumpet will sound, the dead will be raised imperishable, and we will all be changed.*
>
> *1 Corinthians 15:51-52*

Once believers are snatched away they will remain in the presence of the Lord Jesus Christ and appear before the *bema* seat of judgement to receive rewards for faithful service and good works performed since becoming a born again Christian.

> *For what is our hope, our joy, or the crown in which we will glory in the presence of our Lord Jesus when he comes? Is it not you? Indeed you are our glory and joy.*
>
> *1 Thessalonians 2:19-20*

Final Thought

This is not the time to be careless and neglect your salvation. No one should reject the offer of God's unconditional love and his free gift of eternal life. Why would anyone want to deny themselves the opportunity to claim God's promise to have all their sins forgiven and receive the assurance that Jesus Christ will be their friend, comforter and personal saviour?

---

[65] Finis Jennings Dake; *Dake's Annotated Reference Bible;* page 301

How shall we escape if we ignore so great a salvation? This salvation, which was first announced by the Lord, was confirmed to us by those who heard him.

Hebrews 2:3

If you feel challenged and wish to become a born again Christian please turn to the Postscript for further guidance, and say the prayer of salvation that will invite Jesus Christ into your life.

Questions

Why is the person who reads or listens to the reading of the book of Revelation promised a special blessing?

_____

_____

Why has the 21st century church lost the power and zeal of the early apostolic church?

_____

_____

What are the three main threats facing today's church?

_____

_____

_____

To what extent does the ecumenical movement pose a danger to the modern church?

_____

_____

Which of the seven church eras has the most to teach the church of today?

_____

_____

Does a church have to experience hardship, opposition and persecution before it becomes truly evangelical?

_____

_____

CHAPTER ELEVEN

The Failing Churches

Introduction

There are five churches out of the seven churches Jesus Christ audited that we will examine. First, we examine the worst two churches, as Jesus Christ had nothing positive to say about the churches at Sardis and Laodicea which to all outward appearances appeared a success. Jesus Christ is scathing about the church at Sardis which he concludes is "dead" whereas the church at Laodicea he concluded was only "lukewarm".

Having a large congregation, big collections, a full programme of activities and a large worship band are not in themselves a sign of spiritual health. These two churches did not suffer hardship or suffer persecution. Their problem was that their sense of priorities was completely wrong and they had become lukewarm, complacent and spiritually naked.

The Dead Church at Sardis

"To the angel of the church in Sardis write: These are the words of him who holds the seven spirits of God and the seven stars. I know your deeds; you have a reputation of being alive, but you are dead. Wake up! Strengthen what remains and is about to die, for I have found your deeds unfinished in the sight of my God. Remember, therefore, what you have received and heard; hold it fast, and repent. But if you do not wake up, I will come like a thief, and you will not know at what time I will come to you. Yet you have a few people in Sardis who have not soiled their clothes. They will walk with me, dressed in white, for they are worthy. The one who is victorious will, like them, be dressed in white. I will never blot out the name of that person from the book of life, but will

181

acknowledge that name before my Father and his angels. Whoever has ears, let them hear what the Spirit says to the churches."

Revelation 3:1-6

The ancient capital of Lydia was Sardis which means 'those escaping'. Sardis is now known as the town of Sartmustafa. The city of Sardis was the prosperous cultural centre of Asia Minor. It was famous for dyeing delicate woollen fabrics, making carpets, and its ability to refine precious metals.

The church at Sardis had a good reputation as a thriving church in the city, but the church was badly led and poorly organised. It was forever starting new initiatives but failed to follow through with them and as a result never delivered anything worthwhile. Jesus urged the church to stop being complacent but obey his teaching and be faithful. He delivers a devastating verdict: "You have a reputation of being alive, but you are dead. Wake up!" (Rev.3:1-2)

Jesus warns them that unless they "wake up" and repent, he will come unexpectedly "like a thief" (2.Pet.3:10a) and take away what they have. The Greek word *kleptes* means 'a stealer'.[66] The apostle Peter wrote to the church in A.D. 65, after he was imprisoned by Nero and was expecting to be executed. In response to their impatient question, "Where is this 'coming' he promised?" (2.Pet.3:4a) Peter responded:

With the Lord a day is like a thousand years and a thousand years like a day. The Lord is not slow in keeping his promise, as some understand slowness. Instead he is patient with you, not wanting anyone to perish, but everyone to come to repentance.

2 Peter 3:8-9

His warning that the Lord's return will be like a thief coming to steal from them was particularly pertinent to this church, because although the city was well-fortified it had suffered grievous losses following two surprise attacks. It endured a siege before it was conquered by Cyrus the Great, then following the Ionian Revolt the Athenians burned down the city and destroyed it.

---

[66] *Strong's Exhaustive Concordance of the Bible*

Jesus pays tribute to the few people in the church at Sardis who had remained faithful and avoided becoming contaminated by the world and pagan practices. He makes it plain that everybody commences life with their name written in the book of life, but the choices they make subsequently, when they are of an age to decide for themselves, determines whether their name remains or is removed. In the case of the few faithful believers in the church at Sardis, he assures them their names would never be removed from the Book of Life.

> *"The one who is victorious will, like them, be dressed in white. I will never blot out the name of that person from the book of life, but will acknowledge that name before my Father and his angels."*
>
> *Revelation 3:5*

WHAT IS THE LESSON FOR TODAY FROM THE CHURCH AT SARDIS?

Material prosperity, an absence of spiritual opposition or testing or persecution, can lead to complacency. Any church can easily become like the church at Sardis which is merely going through the motions of following Jesus Christ but is actually more concerned with maintaining a good public image. A church can only be active and effective when it concentrates on providing sound teaching and relies on the power of the Holy Spirit. When there is no spiritual depth in its teaching, or an absence of genuine outward signs of love, and no evangelism or outreach is taking place, it can become ineffective and almost spiritually dead.

The Lukewarm Church in Laodicea

> *"To the angel of the church in Laodicea write: These are the words of the Amen, the faithful and true witness, the ruler of God's creation. I know your deeds, that you are neither cold nor hot. I wish you were either one or the other! So, because you are lukewarm – neither hot nor cold – I am about to spit you out of my mouth. You say, 'I am rich; I have acquired wealth and do not need a thing.' But you do not realize that you are wretched, pitiful, poor, blind and naked. I counsel you to buy from me gold refined in the fire, so you can become rich; and white clothes to wear, so you can cover your shameful nakedness; and salve to put on your eyes, so you can*

see. Those whom I love I rebuke and discipline. So be earnest and repent. Here I am! I stand at the door and knock. If anyone hears my voice and opens the door, I will come in and eat with that person, and they with me. To the one who is victorious, I will give the right to sit with me on my throne, just as I was victorious and sat down with my Father on his throne. Whoever has ears, let them hear what the Spirit says to the churches."

Revelation 3:14-22

Laodicea means 'people ruling' and was the ancient capital of Phrygia. It was built by Antiochus who named it after his wife Laodicea and is known today as the city of Denzli. It became a wealthy city due to its financial acumen and enjoyed a good reputation as a producer of high quality woollen fabrics and inexpensive, mass-produced outer garments.

The church at Laodicea was located in a prosperous industrial and commercial centre. It was a wealthy and self-sufficient church but spiritually bankrupt. It was proud to be known as a friendly and welcoming church to its many visitors, although Jesus Christ was not fooled by outward appearances. He saw how superficial, worldly and unspiritual the church was and it made him want to be physically sick. "I am about to spit you out of my mouth." (Rev.3:16)

Outside the city, known as the 'white castle' of Pamukkale, were salty hot springs and this water was piped to Laodicea in a stone aqueduct from the thermal springs which lay 10 km south of the city; a considerable engineering feat! By the time the water reached Laodicea it was lukewarm and acted as an emetic which caused those who drank it to vomit. In contrast, the water to the west in Colossac was refreshingly cold; and the water to the north, at Hierapolis, was hot and medicinally healthy. The city was famous for its medical school and enjoyed a good reputation for its Phrygian eye salve and ear medicine.

Jesus did not have a good word to say about this church. He said there was an urgent need for the church to repent and become holy and righteous. His devastating verdict was that the church was despicable, inadequate, impoverished, unsubstantial and worthless. The church lacked insight and was unable to see any of its faults or prepared to listen to any criticism – which is rather ironic for a city famous for its ear medicine and eye salve!

Jesus said the church of Laodicea was deluded and was only going through the motions of Christianity. There was no enthusiasm to study the Bible, obey its teaching or engage in any form of evangelism. It was a church that had not only compromised its beliefs but had neglected the teaching of Jesus Christ altogether. It was so complacent and hypocritical, the Holy Spirit had deserted the church, but was waiting patiently for the church to repent and invite him back inside.

> *"Here I am! I stand at the door and knock. If anyone hears my voice and opens the door, I will come in and eat with that person, and they with me."*
>
> *Revelation 3:20*

The door to the church, which is also the heart of the unbeliever, can only be opened from the handle located on the inside.

> *I do not think the devil cares how many churches you build, if only you have lukewarm preachers and people in them.*
>
> *Charles Spurgeon* [67]

Jesus said, "Those whom I love I rebuke and discipline. So be earnest and repent." (Rev.3:19) Jesus wants to have fellowship with the church of believers and urges them to repent, then address and correct their shortcomings. His promise to them was conditional: provided they address their shortcomings they can earn the right to be a member of his holy family and enjoy eternal life with him in heaven (see Rev.3:21).

WHAT IS THE LESSON FOR TODAY FROM THE CHURCH AT LAODICEA?

This is the equivalent of today's modern, middle class, well-resourced church with a nicely furnished, purpose-built building, equipped with all the latest electronic and musical instruments. Any church can become complacent and worldly by losing sight of its mission to preach the gospel and encourage its congregation to lead holy and righteous lives. Such a church must repent and completely change its ways before it becomes a hollow shell spiritually. The mistake the church in Laodicea made was to become lukewarm, which made it ineffective and unable to enjoy Jesus Christ's holy presence.

Believers are not to become complacent, but to stand up for the truth of the gospel and witness to their community. Many churches neglect to

---

[67] *www.spurgeon.10000quotes.com*

teach about his suffering on the cross for their sins, the judgement seat of Christ or the reality of hell. Neither is there teaching on living a righteous life or a challenge to be holy, righteous believers, because these topics are uncomfortable for many congregations and leaders to tackle.

The modern church can be guilty of losing their first love and reluctant to conduct evangelism in their local community because it may attract ridicule or even vandalism. It is far easier to be a people-pleaser and attempt to be all things to all people. Keeping quiet to avoid embarrassment compromises the church's mission and fails to challenge the world's standards and values.

> *The present general state of the professing church which is one of lukewarmness is the most hateful and nauseous of any yet described. We may well term the last phase of church history on the eve of judgement, the Christless period.*
>
> Dr S.A. Boreland[68]

The Loveless Church of Ephesus

> *"To the angel of the church in Ephesus write: These are the words of him who holds the seven stars in his right hand and walks among the seven golden lampstands. I know your deeds and your hard work and your perseverance. I know that you cannot tolerate wicked people, that you have tested those who claim to be apostles but are not, and have found them false. You have persevered and have endured hardships for my name, and have not grown weary. Yet I hold this against you: You have forsaken the love you had at first. Consider how far you have fallen! Repent and do the things you did at first. If you do not repent, I will come to you and remove your lampstand from its place. But you have this in your favor: You hate the practices of the Nicolaitans, which I also hate. Whoever has ears, let them hear what the Spirit says to the churches. To the one who is victorious, I will give the right to eat from the tree of life, which is in the paradise of God."*
>
> Revelation 2:1-7

---

[68] *Some Golden Daybreak*

The seven churches were on a circular trade route, situated in modern-day Turkey. The city of Ephesus means 'desired one' or 'beloved'. It was a major port on the Aegean Sea, the gateway to Asia Minor and home to one of the seven wonders of the Ancient World, the temple of Artemis. The city of Ephesus had erected a temple to Diana, which was a Roman version of the pagan Greek god Artemis.

The church at Ephesus is commended for its hard work, perseverance and for rejecting false prophets and had endured hardships for the sake of the gospel. Nevertheless, it remained a failing church because spiritually it had "left thy first love" (Rev.2:4, KJV). The Greek word *alphiemi* means 'an intensive form of forsaking or laying aside'[69].

Over time the church had lost its first love for Jesus Christ, including any enthusiasm to follow his teaching to love one another and seek to reach the unsaved. The Ephesus church did not tolerate evil and loathed the pagan practices of the Nicolaitans and had suffered hardship defending the church against false prophets and apostasy. Jesus invites them to "consider how far you have fallen" (Rev.2:5). Sound teaching and perseverance are not enough without '*agape* love' for Jesus Christ, which is the highest form of love.

The Nicolaitans were considered heretical by mainstream churches as they indulged in sexual practices and incorporated them into their religious ceremonies. Little is known about this group but they had a substantial following in Pergamum and Ephesus. Iranaeus and Hippolytus claim Nicolas was the founder of this sect, who was at one time a convert to Christianity.

> "But you have this in your favor: You hate the practices of the Nicolaitans, which I also hate."
>
> *Revelation 2:6*

The apostle Luke records that Nicolas was one of seven deacons chosen to concentrate on distributing the food to the widows and meeting their welfare needs, freeing the twelve disciples to concentrate on the Great Commission.

> "We will turn this responsibility over to them and will give our attention to prayer and the ministry of the word." This proposal pleased the whole group. They chose Stephen, a man

---

[69] *Strong's Exhaustive Concordance of the Bible*

full of faith and of the Holy Spirit; also Philip, Procorus, Nicanor, Timon, Parmenas, and Nicolas from Antioch, a convert to Judaism.

Acts 6:3b-5

However, Nicolas succumbed to false teaching and founded the Nicolaitan sect which adopted false teaching similar to Balaam and led many members of the church astray (see Rev.2:14-15). Although the church at Ephesus had resisted the wicked practices of the Nicolaitans and expelled false apostles from the church, they had abandoned their initial enthusiasm for serving the Lord. This prompted Jesus Christ to issue this stern warning:

"If you do not repent, I will come to you and remove your lampstand from its place."

Revelation 2:5b

The threat meant that unless they repent, I will remove the flock now under your care to another place and put it under the care of another pastor.

Albert Barnes[70]

This church and others addressed in these letters were ruined and overthrown by heresies and divisions within, so that Mohammedanism prevails and prospers in all those countries which were once the glory of Christendom, their churches being turned into mosques.

Joseph Benson[71]

Sadly, many of these warnings were not heeded and "eventually only a village remained of what was once mighty Ephesus"[72].

WHAT IS THE LESSON FOR TODAY FROM THE CHURCH AT EPHESUS?

A church that prides itself on doctrinal purity at the expense of love for Jesus Christ is seriously flawed and risks being treated in a similar fashion to the church at Laodicea. This means heeding Jesus Christ's

---

[70] *The Barnes Bible Commentary*
[71] *Benson's Commentary on the Old and New Testaments*
[72] Craig S. Keener; *The Bible Background Commentary*

warnings and stopping being indifferent about the sacrifice Jesus made to secure their salvation.

The message for the 21st century church is to obey his commandments: "Love the Lord your God with all your heart and with all your soul and with all your mind." (Matt.22:37)

Jesus Christ warned them he would close the church down altogether if it continued to be unfaithful and such a poor ambassador for his gospel. This salutary warning applies to every church that abandons their love for the redeeming work of Jesus Christ. However, there is an encouraging message of hope for those who take notice of what the Holy Spirit is saying to this and every church. If they are overcomers they will experience eternal life and everlasting happiness in God's heavenly home.

The Compromising Church at Pergamum

> "To the angel of the church in Pergamum write: These are the words of him who has the sharp, double-edged sword. I know where you live – where Satan has his throne. Yet you remain true to my name. You did not renounce your faith in me, not even in the days of Antipas, my faithful witness, who was put to death in your city – where Satan lives. Nevertheless, I have a few things against you: There are some among you who hold to the teaching of Balaam, who taught Balak to entice the Israelites to sin so that they ate food sacrificed to idols and committed sexual immorality. Likewise, you also have those who hold to the teaching of the Nicolaitans. Repent therefore! Otherwise, I will soon come to you and will fight against them with the sword of my mouth. Whoever has ears, let them hear what the Spirit says to the churches. To the one who is victorious, I will give some of the hidden manna. I will also give that person a white stone with a new name written on it, known only to the one who receives it."

Revelation 2:12-17

The city of Pergamum, which means 'married', was the provincial capital of Rome and a major cultural and learning centre located in what is now southern Turkey. It was founded by the warrior Neoptolemus and his wife Andromache, who named the city after her youngest son Pergamus, and is known today as the town of Bergama. It was a rich and wonderful city famous for its inventors and innovators and had a huge library which Mark Anthony gifted to Cleopatra as a symbol of his love. Despite its beauty and wealth it was evil and notorious for pagan practices and one of the first cities in Asia Minor to build a temple to the Roman Emperor Zeus, which made it the centre of the cult. They built a gigantic altar of Zeus, which measured 120 x 112 feet, where the local citizens were expected to worship. The symbol of a serpent was engraved on all its coins and local citizens were seen as disloyal to the state if they did not worship the emperor.

The church at Pergamum was located "where Satan has his throne. Yet you remain true to my name." (Rev.2:13) The church remained faithful even when the righteous Antipas was killed for being "my faithful witness" (Rev.2:3). Antipas was a deacon in the church and was killed during the reign of Roman Emperor Nero in A.D. 54-58 because he would not renounce his faith in Jesus Christ. His punishment was to be placed inside a large brass bull used for holding sacrifices and roasted alive on the altar of Zeus.

Although the church at Pergamum was praised for being faithful despite these strong pagan influences, "There are some among you who hold to the teaching of Balaam, who taught Balak to entice the Israelites to sin so they ate food sacrificed to idols and committed sexual immorality." (Rev.2:14) Some members of the church were immersed in pagan Roman culture and others were following the false teaching of the Nicolaitans (see Rev.2:15).

The close association between these two pagan groups is indicated by the fact the name 'Balaam' in Hebrew has the same meaning as 'Nicolaitans' in the Greek. 'Nicolaitans' is derived from the Greek words *nikan* meaning 'to conquer' and *laos* which means 'people'. The word Balaam is derived from two Hebrew words *bela* which means 'to conquer' and *ha'am* meaning 'people'.

During the time of Moses when Israel was staying in Shittim, the evil prophet Balaam enticed the Israelite men to be unfaithful. They had sexual relations with Moabite women and ate food that had been offered to Baal. "So Israel yoked themselves to the Baal of Peor. And the Lord's anger burned against them." (Num.25:3) God sent a plague to punish the Israelites and told Moses to put to death all those who had participated in the idolatrous worship of Baal. By the time God stopped the plague it had killed 24,000 people (see Num.25:9). God told Moses to send a large army against the Moabites who were completely destroyed. They slaughtered every man, killed every woman who had committed sexual sin with the Israelites, demolished every town the Moabites had made into settlements and took possession of all their livestock and goods. This harsh retribution demonstrates God is a jealous god and finds idolatry loathsome.

> *"Do not worship any other god, for the LORD, whose name is Jealous, is a jealous God."*
>
> *Exodus 34:14*

Jesus warned the church that unless they repented he would come and punish them. The church had tolerated significant theological errors which had gained a foothold and had deceived some members of the congregation.

> *"Repent therefore! Otherwise, I will soon come to you and fight against them with the sword of my mouth."*
>
> *Revelation 2:16*

Compromising the Christian faith with false teaching from other religions is the greatest evil of all, because it is seductive and damages the integrity of the gospel of salvation.

There is encouraging news from Jesus Christ to those who persevere and overcome Satan's efforts to undermine their faith.

> *"To the one who is victorious, I will also give some of the hidden manna. I will give that person a white stone, with a new name written on it, known only to the one who receives it."*
>
> *Revelation 2:17*

During a criminal trial in ancient Greece, a black stone was used by the judge to declare guilt and condemnation and a "white stone" (in Greek *leukos*) signified innocence and pardon.

> *Conquerors in the public games were also given white and black stones with their names in them, which entitled them to be supported the rest of their lives at public expense.*
>
> *Finis Jennings Dake*[73]

---

[73] *Dake's Annotated Reference Bible*

The reward promised for those who overcome temptation and adversity is spiritual food which is the "hidden manna" (in Greek, *krupto*). Jesus said:

> *"I am the living bread that came down from heaven. Whoever eats this bread will live forever."*
>
> John 6:51

WHAT IS THE LESSON FOR TODAY FROM THE CHURCH AT PERGAMUM?

The modern form of spiritual compromise is termed syncretism. This is where attempts are made to reconcile different religions, cultures and schools of thought. The 21st century equivalent is the move by the ecumenical movement to unite all religions in a 'multi-faith' approach which can only lead to theological compromise. The true church must not allow society to dilute its values, its teaching or the integrity of the Bible, by forming an alliance with the apostate church or Eastern religions or the New Age movement.

> *Do not conform to the pattern of this world, but be transformed by the renewing of your mind. Then you will be able to test and approve what God's will is – his good, pleasing and perfect will.*
>
> Romans 12:2

The apostate church denies the major doctrines of Christianity: the virgin birth, the deity of Jesus Christ, his atoning sacrifice for sin, his bodily resurrection and the second advent – the Second Coming of Jesus Christ. Jesus told Nicodemus 2,000 years ago, "I tell you the truth, unless you are born again, you cannot see the Kingdom of God." (Jn.3:3, NLT)

The church has a disappointing history of tolerating compromise over biblical teaching and moral standards. This applies to many churches today who disregard biblical teaching by performing same-sex marriages in the church, or allow the ordination of homosexuals priests and pastors to positions of leadership, or fail to condemn adultery and fornication amongst their congregations. Many 21st century churches dilute God's message of salvation, his intolerance of sin and the warnings of coming judgement to those who reject Jesus Christ, in order not to upset or lose members of their congregations. The apostle Paul prophesied this would happen in the future when he wrote to Timothy, the evangelist and his co-worker.

For the time will come when people will not put up with sound doctrine. Instead, to suit their own desires, they will gather around them a great number of teachers to say what their itching ears want to hear. They will turn their ears away from the truth and turn aside to myths.

2 Timothy 4:3-4

Some churches compromise biblical truth when their praise and worship groups aim to appeal to popular tastes in music at the expense of meaningful and scripturally accurate lyrics.

The Adulterous Church at Thyatira

"To the angel of the church in Thyatira write: These are the words of the Son of God, whose eyes are like blazing fire and whose feet are like burnished bronze. I know your deeds, your love and faith, your service and perseverance, and that you are now doing more than you did at first. Nevertheless, I have this against you: You tolerate that woman Jezebel, who calls herself a prophet. By her teaching she misleads my servants into sexual immorality and the eating of food sacrificed to idols. I have given her time to repent of her immorality, but she is unwilling. So I will cast her on a bed of suffering, and I will make those who commit adultery with her suffer intensely, unless they repent of her ways. I will strike her children dead. Then all the churches will know that I am he who searches hearts and minds, and I will repay each of you according to your deeds. Now I say to the rest of you in Thyatira, to you who do not hold to her teaching and have not learned Satan's so-called deep secrets, 'I will not impose any other burden on you, except to hold on to what you have until I come.' To the one who is victorious and does my will to the end, I will give authority over the nations - that one 'will rule them with an iron scepter and will dash them to pieces like pottery' – just as I have received authority from my Father. I will also give that one the morning star. Whoever has ears, let them hear what the Spirit says to the churches."

Revelation 2:18-29

The city of Thyatira, meaning 'a perpetual sacrifice', is known today as Akhisar. It was a wealthy city founded by Alexander the Great and established a reputation as a trading centre known for its purple dye. Lydia, one of Paul's converts, was "a dealer in purple cloth" (Acts.16:14).

Jesus said of the church at Thyatira, he was aware of their good works, their love, their faithful service and perseverance, which he gave them credit for "doing more than they did at first" (Rev.2:19). However, Jesus condemns the church for tolerating the false prophetess Jezebel whose false teaching had persuaded faithful members of the congregation to commit fornication and eat food sacrificed to idols. Eating food sacrificed to idols meant going to the temple to receive that food and being exposed to sexual temptation.

When Ahab became king of Israel he was more evil than previous rulers and made God very angry. Ahab permitted the worshipping of false gods throughout the land when he married Jezebel, a zealous Baal-worshipper and "the daughter of Ethbaal king of the Sidonians, and began to serve Baal and worship him" (1.Kgs.16:31). Ahab built a temple with an altar to Baal in Samaria (see 1.Kgs.16:32) and also "made an Asherah pole" (1.Kgs.16:33), which was a sacred tree or pole which honoured the Ugaritic mother goddess of Asherah. These actions "did more to arouse the anger of the LORD, the God of Israel, than did all the kings of Israel before him" (1.Kgs.16:33). Elijah told Ahab that God would withhold the dew and the rain. The terrible drought that followed caused famine throughout the land for the next three years (see 1.Kgs.18:1). Jezebel imported nine hundred false Baal prophets which firmly established idolatry in the land because "Jezebel was killing off the Lord's prophets" (1.Kgs.18:4).

The threat Jezebel posed was so great that Elijah confronted King Ahab about abandoning God's commandments and worshipping Baal. He challenged the people at Mount Carmel to decide whom they would serve: "If the LORD is God, follow him; but if Baal is God, follow him." (1.Kgs.18:21b) The test was for Elijah and the prophets of Baal to sacrifice a bull to their god. Elijah would rely completely on God to send "a consuming fire" (Deut.4:24) to burn up his offering. The false prophets called to Baal throughout the day to send fire, but without success, and Elijah, who had complete confidence in God, began to taunt them.

So they shouted louder and slashed themselves with swords and spears, as was their custom, until their blood flowed. Midday passed, and they continued their frantic prophesying until the time for the evening sacrifice. But there was no response, no one answered, no one paid any attention.

1 Kings 18:28-29

Finally, when there was no response from Baal they gave up and it was Elijah's turn. First, Elijah thoroughly drenched the offering on the altar three times with water and then he prayed to the Lord.

"Answer me, LORD, answer me, so these people will know that you, LORD, are God, and that you are turning their hearts back again." Then the fire of the LORD fell and burned up the sacrifice, the wood, the stones and the soil, and also licked up the water in the trench. When all the people saw this they fell prostrate and cried, "The LORD – he is God! The LORD – he is God!"

1 Kings 18:37-39

Following this demonstration of God's mighty power, Elijah ordered the people to seize all the prophets of Baal and they killed them in the Kishon Valley. When Jezebel heard what had happened she was furious and swore to kill Elijah, who was so scared he ran away to Beersheba and hid in the wilderness.

Jesus told the church at Thyatira that because Jezebel is unrepentant she will suffer judgement and there will be serious consequences for her, her children and followers.

"I will cast her on a bed of suffering, and I will make those who commit adultery with her suffer intensely, unless they repent of her ways."

Revelation 2:22

Jesus reminds the church it has been given ample opportunity to repent and unless they demonstrate genuine repentance, terrible judgement will follow. This is a warning to every church, including those in the 21st century, that believers will only be rewarded according to their righteous actions.

Jesus promised all those in Thyatira that he would not make further demands on them "except to hold on to what you have until I come"

(Rev.2:25) and become overcomers. If they did this they would receive eternal life and take part in Christ's divine rule and have positions of leadership and authority in the Millennium.

Christians can easily be led astray by cults, occult practices and false teaching if they do not have a thorough knowledge of the Bible. "Satan's so-called deep secrets" (Rev.2:24) are "mystery cults which have deep secrets shared only among the initiates"[74]. They are not "deep secrets" to Jesus Christ, who is well aware of the lies and deceitful ways Satan uses to deceive the church. One of Satan's ploys is the seductive but false teaching that salvation can be obtained by good works alone.

> *For it is by grace you have been saved, through faith – and this is not from yourselves, it is the gift of God – not by works, so that no one can boast.*
>
> *Ephesians 2:8-9*

It is unwise to explore the depths of Satan secrets, as that is a road to bondage and darkness. Paul tells us to focus on the light and concentrate on becoming holy and righteous.

> *Finally brothers and sisters, whatever is true, whatever is noble, whatever is right, whatever is pure, whatever is lovely, whatever is admirable – if anything is excellent or praiseworthy – think about such things.*
>
> *Philippians 4:8*

WHAT IS THE LESSON FOR TODAY FROM THE CHURCH AT THYATIRA?

Christians and believers need to stay alert to avoid compromising and deserting their faith by being lured into false teaching. The prosperity gospel, counterfeit healing ministries and those that perform false signs and wonders must be resisted. There are many false religions and sects active today which attempt to entice Christians into apostasy, idolatry and unholy lifestyles. All forms of apostasy must be firmly resisted by Christians who wish to share in the kingdom of God. Those who faithfully persevere in their Christian faith and are victorious will have important responsibilities serving in Jesus Christ's divine Millennial Reign over all the nations.

---

[74] Craig S. Keener; *The Bible Background Commentary*

Points for Reflection

Each letter to these five churches identifies the triumphs and failings of them all. It should act as a wake-up call to churches in the 21st century to examine themselves in a spirit of humility and ask themselves, are we like one of these churches? These assessments conducted by Jesus Christ are prophetic and sound an alert to all churches to the deceitful ways of the devil.

> *"For false Christs and false prophets will appear and they will provide great signs and wonders, so as to deceive, if possible, even the elect (God's chosen ones). Listen carefully, I have told you in advance."*

Matthew 24:24-25 (AMP)

Jesus had nothing positive to say about the churches at Sardis and Laodicea. His verdict on the church at Sardis was it is "dead"; and the church at Laodicea was even worse – it is "lukewarm" and makes him want to be sick. The churches at Ephesus, Pergamum and Thyatira are told to reflect on how far they have fallen spiritually and to mend their ways. They are warned a time is coming when it will be too late to repent. Many churches, whilst biblically faithful to the gospel, fail to wholeheartedly practise care and love for each other. We are reminded that faithfulness and obedience are more important to Jesus Christ than anything else.

Questions

How can a believer protect themselves against being deceived by false teachers and false prophets?

_____

_____

Should a believer continue to support a church where the leader is in a same-sex marriage or relationship?

_____

_____

How can a believer make a stand against fornication, transgender relationships, underage sex, pornography and abortion?

_____

_____

Are the dangers associated with materialism and complacency the greatest threat to an effective church today?

_____

_____

Why do many church's thrive when they suffer persecution but risk becoming ineffective when they don't?

_____

_____

Why does the church have so little to say publicly about the evils facing society today?

_____

_____

CHAPTER TWELVE

The Victorious Churches

Introduction

The two churches that received fulsome praise were Smyrna and Philadelphia, who had suffered persecution but remained faithful. They did not compromise their faith but enthusiastically followed the teaching of Jesus Christ and lived holy lives.

The Suffering Church at Smyrna

"To the angel of the church in Smyrna write: These are the words of him who is the First and the Last, who died and came to life again. I know your afflictions and your poverty – yet you are rich! I know about the slander of those who say they are Jews and are not, but are a synagogue of Satan. Do not be afraid of what you are about to suffer. I tell you, the devil will put some of you in prison to test you, and you will suffer persecution for ten days. Be faithful, even to the point of death, and I will give you life as your victor's crown. Whoever has ears, let them hear what the Spirit says to the churches. The one who is victorious will not be hurt at all by the second death. Whoever has ears, let them hear what the Spirit says to the churches."

Revelation 2:8-11

Smyrna, meaning 'myrrh', is known as the city of Izmir today. Smyrna was a bustling seaport, home to Homer and the temple of Athens. The church at Smyrna was located in an area of deprivation where satanic influences were very powerful. The church remained faithful and exercised courage in the face of opposition and persecution. Jesus told them he appreciated they had suffered persecution and poverty, but considered they were spiritually wealthy (see Rev.2:11). This church was

199

poor materially but was generous, sharing its few resources with those who were in greater need; furthermore they were willing to pay whatever it cost to follow Jesus Christ. The church at Smyrna received nothing but praise from Jesus Christ because it remained faithful and spiritually alive under adverse circumstances.

The church was home to a large Jewish community who were hostile to Christianity and made slanderous accusations against the church, which exacerbated the persecution the church received from the Roman authorities. It was held up as an example of excellence because it remained faithful despite being tested and placed under great pressure. Jesus warned the church to be ready for further testing, including imprisonment for some members of the congregation, warning them further persecution would follow. The believers at Smyrna were promised they would receive the gift of eternal life and wear a Victor's Crown, if they continued to remain faithful, even though it may cost them their lives. This suffering would include false imprisonment, which they should consider a test of their faith by Satan. Jesus warned the church at Smyrna, "You will suffer persecution for ten days." (Rev.2:10)

After God rescued the Israelites from slavery at the hands of the Egyptians they rebelled and treated God with contempt, so he declared, "For forty years – one year for each of the forty days you explored the land – you will suffer for your sins and know what it is like to have me against you." (Num.14:34)

When God made Ezekiel the prophet "a watchman for the people of Israel" (Ez.3:17) he put the sins of the people onto Ezekiel and assigned him "the same number of days as the years of their sin. So for 390 days you will bear the sin of the people of Israel." (Ez.4:5) The parallel with God asking Jesus to suffer death on the cross for the sins of the whole of mankind is unmistakable.

Over the following centuries thousands of Christians were persecuted and martyred for their faith in the city of Smyrna, as was prophesied. There was a severe persecution for Christians, in particular, which lasted for ten years, when Emperor Diocetian banned Christianity in A.D. 303 and publicly burned the scriptures and established emperor worship. Ten years later, in A.D. 313, Constantine and Lionius granted Christians freedom to practice their religion once again.

The testing of the church at Smyrna is a reminder of the initial testing Daniel, Hananiah, Mishael and Azariah experienced during the reign of Nebuchadnezzar, after he conquered Jerusalem. The king appointed

Ashpenaz his chief court official, to arrange for outstanding physical specimens of manhood from amongst the Israelites' royal family to serve in the king's palace. After three years of training they would enter the Babylonian king's service. Having been selected, Nebuchadnezzar's chief official Aspenaz gave them new Babylonian names: Belteshazzar, Shadrach, Meshach and Abednego respectively (see Dan.1:7).

Daniel decided at the outset they would remain faithful to God and obey his dietary laws by keeping to a Jewish diet rather than eat and drink the rich, unholy food and wine provided in the palace. Ashpenaz was afraid he would suffer the king's displeasure and risk losing his life so he told them, "Why should he see you looking worse than the other young men your age?" (Dan.1:10b) However, Daniel persuaded him to allow them to test out his healthy eating diet.

> *"Please test your servants for ten days: Give us nothing but vegetables to eat and water to drink. Then compare our appearance with that of the young men who eat the royal food, and treat your servants in accordance with what you see."*
>
> *Daniel 1:12-13*

The outcome of the test was they looked healthier and better nourished than the young men who had followed the diet of the royal household, so Aspenaz allowed them to continue their Jewish diet. At the end of their period of training, when questioned by Nebuchadnezzar, he found their knowledge, understanding, wisdom and intellectual prowess "ten times better than all the magicians and enchanters in his whole kingdom" (Dan.1:20).

This was the first test alluded to in relation to the church at Smyrna but a significant test of faith because, as with Daniel, it demonstrated their character. Overcoming small obstacles as the church at Smyrna had done was evidence they would be likely to stand their ground when faced with a severe test of their faith.

The ultimate test for Shadrach, Meshach and Abednego came later.

> *"We want you to know, Your Majesty, that we will not serve your gods or worship the image of gold you have set up."*
>
> *Daniel 3:18*

Nebuchadnezzar constructed an enormous gold-covered statue ninety feet high and nine feet wide on the plain of Dura which dominated the landscape of Mesopotamia. Even when threatened with certain death these three faithful men refused to bow down and worship his pagan idol. When Nebuchadnezzar heard of their disobedience he was "furious with rage" (Dan.3:13) and had them "bound and thrown into the blazing furnace" (Dan.3:21) which he heated to seven times the normal temperature. The outcome astonished King Nebuchadnezzar.

> *"Look! I see four men walking around in the fire, unbound and unharmed and the fourth looks like a son of the gods."*
>
> *Daniel 3:25*

WHAT IS THE LESSON FOR TODAY FROM THE CHURCH AT SMYRNA?

A church that stands its ground when its faith is tested over minor doctrinal or moral issues will be prepared to stand their ground when major issues and persecution arises. Faithfulness and obedience to Jesus Christ's teaching and commandments is of great importance to him. All Christians who remain faithful and do not compromise the Truth will receive eternal life and rewards in heaven.

The Faithful Church at Philadelphia

> *"To the angel of the church in Philadelphia write: These are the words of him who is holy and true, who holds the key of David. What he opens no one can shut, and what he shuts no one can open. I know your deeds. See, I have placed before you an open door that no one can shut. I know that you have little strength, yet you have kept my word and have not denied my name. I will make those who are of the synagogue of Satan, who claim to be Jews though they are not, but are liars – I will make them come and fall down at your feet and acknowledge that I have loved you. Since you have kept my command to endure patiently, I will also keep you from the hour of trial that is going to come on the whole world to test the inhabitants of the earth. I am coming soon. Hold on to what you have, so that no one will take your crown."*
>
> *Revelation 3:7-11*

The city of Philadelphia, which means 'brotherly love', is nowadays known as Alasehir. It was known as the 'Gateway to the East' and renowned for its grapes, textiles and leather goods.

At first glance this appears to be an unimpressive church with very limited resources, as it only had a shabby building for its small congregation to worship in. However, Jesus has nothing but unqualified praise for its faithfulness and perseverance in overcoming difficulties and challenges. The church in Philadelphia, like the church at Smyrna, had been expelled from the synagogue, but Jesus said they were his special chosen people because they faithfully followed his teaching and shared the gospel message enthusiastically.

The church has stood firm and been resolute in defending the true gospel of Jesus Christ and remained a loving, evangelical fellowship.

> *"What he opens no one can shut, and what he shuts no one can open. I know your deeds. See I have placed before you an open door that no one can shut."*
>
> *Revelation 3:7-8*

The faithful church at Philadelphia is commended for patiently suffering unfair and slanderous treatment by those it would expect to be its friends. Jesus promises to humble the hypocritical, deceitful Jews and compel them to show deference and respect to this faithful and admiral church. Jesus loves these believers and holds up this assembly as a shining example to all other churches.

> *"I will make those who are of the synagogue of Satan, who claim to be Jews though they are not, but are liars – I will make them come and fall down at your feet and acknowledge that I love you."*
>
> *Revelation 3:9*

The city of Philadelphia was well-known for holding the Greek Games where the winner would receive the prize (*brabion* in the Greek), which was a crown (*stephonas* in the Greek). This example is used to encourage the church to persevere with their faithful witness because if they do, they can expect to receive the reward of a crown in heaven.

> *"Hold on to what you have, so that no one will take your crown."*
>
> *Revelation 3:11*

Jesus also promised the church, "Since you have kept my command to endure patiently, I will also keep you from the hour of trial that is going to come on the whole world, to test the inhabitants of the earth."

(Rev.3:10) This is a reference to the Tribulation and a wonderful promise that the Rapture of the Church will occur before the time of Tribulation turns the whole world into chaos and confusion.

Jesus said this church will become an open door for evangelism and ministry because of its exemplary record. This demonstrates that when a church places following the teaching of Jesus Christ at the centre of all it does, then everything else falls into place. The church at Philadelphia is promised an important role when God establishes the new heaven and the new earth, as they will be a pillar in the new Jerusalem.

> *"The one who is victorious I will make a pillar in the temple of My God. Never again will they leave it. I will write on them the name of my God and the name of the city of my God; the new Jerusalem, which is coming down out of heaven from my God; and I will also write on them my new name."*
>
> Revelation 3:12-13

WHAT IS THE LESSON FOR TODAY FROM THE CHURCH AT PHILADELPHIA?

This church should not judge itself by focusing on numbers in membership or the healthy state of its finances. It should recognise that fruit and blessing comes to a church of believers that perseveres faithfully, despite opposition and persecution. The church must not dilute or compromise the teaching of the word of God but concentrate on winning lost souls for his kingdom. Jesus promises all believers that if they persevere in proclaiming the truth they will receive their rewards when he returns.

> *"Look, I am coming soon! My reward is with me, and I will give to each person according to what they have done."*
>
> Revelation 22:12

The church at Philadelphia is a model for every church in the 21st century. Jesus Christ will be returning soon but without warning, and the church must be vigilant and proactive while they wait expectantly for his return.

Points for Reflection

Jesus always tries to encourage believers in the churches to serve him faithfully. He is always delighted when the church can demonstrate it has the following qualities:

- faithfully following biblical teaching and obeying all God's commandments;
- standing firm and being a faithful witness to the unsaved;
- continuing to be enthusiastic about biblical Truths;
- showing love to others and doing good deeds;
- working hard and demonstrating perseverance;
- rejecting false prophets, teachers and those who worship false gods;
- patiently suffering unfair treatment, enduring hardship and persecution;
- avoiding the influence of evil and wicked people;
- resisting pressure to compromise the teaching of Jesus with false religions;
- refusing to conform to the world's standards;
- living righteous and holy lives.

All believers who are living holy and righteous lives in churches that are standing firm and being faithful to the word of God, are a delight to Jesus Christ.

A Closing Thought

Jesus Christ wants every church and every believer to be a "conqueror" (Rev.3:12, NRSV) an "overcomer" (KJV/AMP) and "victorious" (NIV/NLT). All believers who persevere and who are victorious are promised a reward in heaven by Jesus Christ.

> *So do not throw away your confidence; it will be richly rewarded. You need to persevere so that when you have done the will of God, you will receive what he has promised. For, "In just a little while, he who is coming will come and will not delay."*
>
> *Hebrews 10:36-37*

205

Questions

Is the desire for a 'multi-faith' approach a path that leads to compromising biblical Truth?

_____

_____

_____

What should a believer do if they cannot find a church which measures up to the standards of the church at Smyrna and Philadelphia?

_____

_____

_____

In 'Points for Reflection' we have identified eleven qualities a church should possess. Which do you think are the most important?

_____

_____

Can you place the eleven qualities a church should possess in order of priority?

_____   _____

_____   _____

_____   _____

_____   _____

_____   _____

_____

Does the church you attend meet the criteria set out in 'Points for Reflection'?

_____

_____

_____

When should a believer prayerfully consider changing their church?

_____

_____

_____

POSTSCRIPT

How to Become a Christian

This poem entitled *In Troubled Times* by Gillian Rickards highlights the struggles we all face in life. There is no need to struggle on your own if you become born again and accept Jesus Christ as your personal Saviour.

My child you know I love you, and I want you just to be
Content to feel the blessings I will bestow on thee.
My child I know you love me, as you stand before me now,
I also know you struggle, you often ask me how.

How can I win the battles that rage so deep within?
How do I stop the deep despair Father, where do I begin?
Just lean upon my shoulder, put your hand into my hand,
I'll lead you through your troubles and I'll help you make a stand.

I'm there just waiting for you, to give all your life to me,
I'm there to take your burden, I'll set your spirit free.
You are so very precious and I will touch your life,
So, give me all your troubles and give me all your strife.

My peace will fall upon you, my love will hold you fast,
Your burden will be lighter, just rest in me and ask
As we tread my path together, everything will be made new,
You can rest upon my promise I'll do this just for you. [75]

---

[75] Reproduced by kind permission of Gillian Richards

How Can I Become a Christian?

If you have been challenged by Gillian's poem and by what you have read about God's plan for the future, you may be asking, how can I become a Christian?

There are three simple steps to do this:

A real Christian is someone who has a personal relationship with God by inviting Jesus to become their Lord and Saviour.

STEP 1:   Admit that you have sinned by falling short of God's standard – admit you need a Saviour to deal with your past and assure your future.

STEP 2:   Believe that Jesus is the Son of God who died on the Cross to pay the penalty for your sins.

STEP 3:   Receive Jesus as Saviour and Lord of your life by personal invitation and ask His forgiveness for your sins.

Your decision to receive Christ as Saviour and Lord is the most important decision you will ever make. Here is a prayer you can pray – if you can find a quiet place to quietly pray this aloud:

Lord Jesus,

I believe you are the Son of God. I believe you died on the Cross for me. I am sorry for my sins and I truly want to turn away from them. I ask you to forgive me and cleanse my heart.

[Pause here to mention anything on your conscience. Take your time, then continue.]

I want to trust you with my life, starting right now. Please be my Lord and Saviour. I invite you into my life. Please help me to live by the power of the Holy Spirit, to guide and to teach me.

I now believe your promise in the Bible that I am born again. I am a true child of God. Help me to trust you with all my heart. Thank you, Lord Jesus.

Amen.

If you prayed those words from your heart, you can be sure that God heard you.[76]

If you prayed that prayer and would like to receive a free copy of the New Testament and Psalms, please send an email to:

stevegravett2@gmail.com

---

[76] Reprinted with permission from *Voice* magazine: Full Gospel Businessmen UK & Ireland

Bibliography

Boreland, Dr S. A.; *Some Golden Daybreak*

Dake, Finnis Jennings; *Dake's Annotated Reference Bible*

Hinson, Ed & Ice, Thomas; *Charting the Bible Chronologically*

Jones, David; *The Coming Bride*

Jones, Rev. W. Bryon; *The Millennial Reign of Christ*

Keener, Craig S.; *The Bible Background Commentary*

Kinley, Jeff; *As it Was in the Days of Noah*

LaHaye, Tim; *Revelation Unveiled*

LaHaye, Tim & Hindson, Ed; *The Popular Bible Prophecy Commentary*

LaHaye, Tim & Ice, Thomas; *Charting the End Times*

Marshall, Derek; *The Rapture of the Church*

Rhodes, Ron; *Unmasking the Antichrist*

Scofield, Rev. C. I.; *The Scofield Reference Bible (Authorised Version)*

Strong, James; *Strong's Exhaustive Concordance of the Bible*

Taylor, Rev. Glyn; *One World Religion*

Tsarfati, Amir; *The Day Approaching*

Yonggi Cho, Paul; *Revelation*

Also by the Author

Challenging Issues for Christians
ISBN: 9781912821617
Tricorn Books

What are the consequences of backsliding? Why do some Christians think God's commandments are not mandatory? How certain are you about your eternal destination? These questions and many more are tackled in this Bible-based book which challenges Christians to maintain a strong faith and develop successful strategies to tackle the spiritual battles and temptations we all face in these unusual and uncertain days.

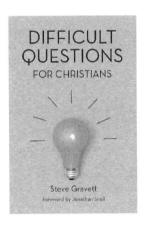

Difficult Questions for Christians
ISBN: 978-1-78815-560-1
Onwards and Upwards Publishers

Are Christians really any different from everyone else? Can assisted suicide ever be justified? Does God bless gay marriage? Steve Gravatt tackles these and other difficult questions head on, believing that when empowered, each of us can gain a better understanding of some of the more challenging issues in our churches. *Difficult Questions for Christians* will empower you in your faith and give you the tools to communicate God's Truth effectively.

Professional Books

The Right Way To Write Reports; Elliot Right Way Books (1998)

Manging Your Boss and Colleagues; How To Books (2000)

Drugs in Prison: A Practitioners' Guide to Penal Policy and Practice in HMPS; Continuum (2000)

Coping With Prison: A Guide to Practitioners on the Realities of Imprisonment; Cassell & Continuum (1999)